"This book will prepare you to recognize and counter deception not only in politics, religion, media and science but especially in yourself."

Hugh Ross, astrophysicist; founder and president,
Reasons to Believe

"I have had the privilege of teaching Bible eschatology at well-known seminaries and churches across the nation. Chuck Pierce and Alemu Beeftu's critically important emphasis on disarming deception makes the truth riveting, communicates sound doctrine and is never boring. You have made the truth come alive! *The Military Guide to Disarming Deception* is a must-read for laypeople as well as an incredible book for pastors to read along with their congregations!"

Dr. Paul McGuire, bestselling author

"We live at a time when deception is absolutely rampant. My hope is that this book will serve as a light in the darkness to multitudes of people. David and Troy share powerful scriptural principles in these pages, and I encourage everyone to get *The Military Guide to Disarming Deception* and to share it with their family and friends. We truly are living in the end times, and the level of deception in our society is only going to get worse.

Michael Snyder, founder, The Economic Collapse Blog;
nationally syndicated writer and media personality

"*The Military Guide to Disarming Deception* is a summoning to the courageous and faithful disciples of our Lord. It skillfully shows how to pick up the sword of the Spirit and put on the whole armor of God, which is to put on Christ as our vestments of battle armor."

Rev. Kevin Jessip, founder and president, The Return, The
Renewal and the Global Strategic Alliance

"What I truly appreciate about *The Military Guide to Disarming Deception* is the detail the authors offer regarding how militaries actually operate to destroy their enemy and how as Christians we must learn these same tactics to defeat our enemies. Their descriptions about deception and indoctrination are eye-opening! Their discussion on complacency and subversion should be enough to motivate any true man or woman of God to action."

Paul E. Pickern, executive director,
All Pro Pastors International

"Jesus told His disciples, 'Beware that no one deceives you' (see Matthew 24:4). We live in a world saturated with deception and lies. There is an all-out assault on truth striving to control our everyday lives. We need a strategy to combat and expose the plan of the enemy. *The Military Guide to Disarming Deception* is exactly that. A winning strategy is a battle we all face and cannot afford to lose."

Matt Hagee, lead pastor, Cornerstone Church

"Deception is a military tactic and the master deceiver uses it to wage war. This book shows us how to avoid these snares and stand firm against his lies and deception."

Jimmy Evans, host, *The Tipping Point*

"David Giammona and Troy Anderson do a masterful job of pairing Scripture with modern military warfare that brings the Bible to life. I was educated, entertained and encouraged by their insights and the warnings that come straight from God's Word."

Ken Harrison, chairman, Promise Keepers

"Over the course of history, deception has been an essential tool in warfare. In order to have Issachar wisdom to discern the way we and our nation should go, we must have spiritual tools to cut through the fog of spiritual war to achieve godly perspective, right actions and true freedom. In *The Military Guide for Disarming Deception*, Colonel David Giammona and Troy Anderson have given us an essential resource—the arsenal we need to successfully navigate our prevailing culture of deception and be confident and victorious spiritual warriors."

Major General Bob Dees, U.S. Army, retired; president,
National Center for Healthy Veterans

"I believe deception has given rise to another gospel. Modern media and secularism have caused many to become lukewarm, and as such, many are being deceived. In *The Military Guide to Disarming Deception*, Colonel David Giammona and Troy Anderson prepare the Church with practical and spiritual tactics, techniques and procedures to help us navigate and discern the perilous times we are living in. Every believer must have this book in their last-day's library to be battle ready!"

Jim Bakker, founder, PTL Television Network;
host, *The Jim Bakker Show*

"Giammona and Anderson have done it again! They have put together a masterpiece that will inform, enlighten and challenge your beliefs regarding deception in the end times. This is a must-have book that will guide through the maze of deceit that has blinded the world and confused the Church."

Dr. Thomas R. Horn, founder and CEO, SkyWatch TV

"*The Military Guide to Disarming Deception* pulls out all the stops and takes off the blinders for many who are in the midst of chaos and confusion. In a time of darkness and anxiety, Col. David Giammona and Troy Anderson have done the research and work for you! Every chapter is chock-full of scriptural insight, wisdom and knowledge that will guide you through the night and into the glorious light of His presence."

Rabbi Jonathan Bernis, president and CEO, Jewish Voice
Ministries International

THE
MILITARY
GUIDE TO
DISARMING
DECEPTION

THE MILITARY GUIDE TO DISARMING DECEPTION

BATTLEFIELD TACTICS TO EXPOSE THE ENEMY'S LIES AND TRIUMPH IN TRUTH

COL. DAVID J. GIAMMONA
AND TROY ANDERSON

Chosen

a division of Baker Publishing Group
Minneapolis, Minnesota

© 2022 by David J. Giammona and Troy Anderson

Published by Chosen Books
11400 Hampshire Avenue South
Minneapolis, Minnesota 55438
www.chosenbooks.com

Chosen Books is a division of
Baker Publishing Group, Grand Rapids, Michigan

Library of Congress Cataloging-in-Publication Data
Names: Giammona, David J., author. | Anderson, Troy (Journalist), author.
Title: The military guide to disarming deception : battlefield tactics to expose the enemy's lies and triumph in truth / Col. David J. Giammona and Troy Anderson.
Description: Minneapolis, Minnesota : Chosen Books, a division of Baker Publishing Group, [2022] | Includes bibliographical references.
Identifiers: LCCN 2022004195 | ISBN 9780800762582 (paperback) | ISBN 9780800762988 (casebound) | ISBN 9781493437528 (ebook)
Subjects: LCSH: Spiritual warfare. | Deception. | Discernment (Christian theology)
Classification: LCC BV4509.5 .G4665 2022 | DDC 235/.4—dc23/eng/20220302
LC record available at https://lccn.loc.gov/2022004195

Unless otherwise indicated, Scripture quotations are from THE HOLY BIBLE, NEW INTERNATIONAL VERSION®, NIV® Copyright © 1973, 1978, 1984, 2011 by Biblica, Inc.® Used by permission. All rights reserved worldwide.

Scripture quotations labeled BSB are from the Berean Bible (www.Berean.Bible), Berean Study Bible (BSB) © 2016–2020 by Bible Hub and Berean.Bible. Used by permission. All rights reserved.

Scripture quotations marked CSB have been taken from the Christian Standard Bible®, copyright © 2017 by Holman Bible Publishers. Used by permission. Christian Standard Bible® and CSB® are federally registered trademarks of Holman Bible Publishers.

Scripture quotations labeled ESV are from The Holy Bible, English Standard Version® (ESV®), copyright © 2001 by Crossway, a publishing ministry of Good News Publishers. Used by permission. All rights reserved. ESV Text Edition: 2016

Scripture quotations labeled MEV are from The Holy Bible, Modern English Version. Copyright © 2014 by Military Bible Association. Published and distributed by Charisma House.

Scripture quotations labeled NASB are from the (NASB®) New American Standard Bible®, Copyright © 1960, 1971, 1977, 1995, 2020 by The Lockman Foundation. Used by permission. All rights reserved. www.lockman.org

Scripture quotations labeled NKJV are from the New King James Version®. Copyright © 1982 by Thomas Nelson. Used by permission. All rights reserved.

Scripture quotations labeled NLT taken from the Holy Bible, New Living Translation, copyright © 1996, 2004, 2015 by Tyndale House Foundation. Used by permission of Tyndale House Publishers, Inc., Carol Stream, Illinois 60188. All rights reserved.

Cover design by Rob Williams, InsideOut Creative Arts, Inc.

The authors are represented by Alive Communications, Inc.

Baker Publishing Group publications use paper produced from sustainable forestry practices and post-consumer waste whenever possible.

22 23 24 25 26 27 28   7 6 5 4 3 2 1

To my beautiful wife, Esther, my partner in life for the past forty-two years. Your inspiration, late-night talks and dedication to duty have inspired and supported me all these years, and I look forward to more to come. Also, to my three awesome children, Micah, Catarina and Melissa, and their God-given superb spouses, Andrea, Andrew and Luis, and now seven wonderful grandchildren. I am truly blessed.

—David

To my beautiful and warm-hearted wife, Irene, whose encouragement, prayers and excellent work creating the website, videos and graphics for Battle Ready Ministries has been a continual source of inspiration for our readers, ministry followers and board of advisors. I also dedicate this book to our charming and amazing daughters, Marlee and Ashley. The Lord is beyond good and "is able to do immeasurably more than all we ask or imagine, according to his power that is at work within us" (Ephesians 3:20).

—Troy

Contents

PART 3 PERSONAL DECEPTION

Foreword

It is no secret that deception today is running rampant throughout the earth.

When Jesus Christ's disciples asked Him two thousand years ago about "the sign of your coming and of the end of the age," He told them, "Watch out that no one deceives you" (Matthew 24:3–4).

I am convinced that *The Military Guide to Disarming Deception* by Colonel David Giammona and Pulitzer Prize–nominated investigative journalist Troy Anderson will help you and your family not only stand firm against the lies of the enemy in the last days, but also discern and combat the propaganda, disinformation and deceptive ideologies that have infiltrated the Church and society.

This is a life-changing, hard-hitting and deeply insightful book that will help you rise in confident biblical assurance, applying military and spiritual intelligence disciplines to your life, to become an on-fire disciple of Christ and soldier in the army of the Lord.

Today the forces of darkness are amassing in battle array. Satan and his hordes know their time is short; and as the last days approach, they are pulling out all the stops, not just to deceive the world but to bring deception to the Church. They are launching an all-out attack against the Word of God and the Church.

Never in history has there been so critical a time for us to understand God's Word and to prepare ourselves and our loved ones for the war against the people of God.

I am concerned that many will be swept away by the deception and lies the enemy is using to set the global stage for the Antichrist, the false prophet and the mark of the Beast economic system.

As the New World Order approaches, it is time for a new paradigm as God prepares us for spiritual battle in the end times. This book is one of the key tools God is using to keep us informed, ready and triumphant. There are no better experts to show us the way than Giammona and Anderson. Their riveting book will provide you with the biblical keys to engage the enemy with the weapons of our warfare (see 2 Corinthians 10:4), helping you walk in the unstoppable and miraculous power and protection of the Holy Spirit in an age of deceit and confusion.

As I read through the book, I was struck by how the military prepares its forces for the deceptive tactics of its enemies. It is no different for the Church. We need to be armed to fight our spiritual enemies and the extreme propaganda and other deceptions now upon us. This book gives you insights, knowledge and practical exercises at the end of every chapter that you and your family will need to disarm deception and lawlessness.

This book is a powerful follow-on to the national bestseller by Giammona and Anderson—*The Military Guide to Armageddon: Battle-Tested Strategies to Prepare Your Life and Soul for the End Times*. Dramatic and cataclysmic events are unfolding on planet earth in these end times.

Make no mistake about it. Because we are at war with powerful forces of darkness, we no longer have the luxury to sit back and watch from the sidelines. Preachers need to reassess their worldview and messages to call their followers to action. Believers need to reevaluate their lives in light of eternity and the impact they must have on this lost and dying world.

Read this book to be changed, inspired, stimulated and, most of all, challenged. If you are like me, you will not want to put it down before absorbing every word.

As plagues, pestilences, wars and rumors of war run throughout this world, we need new direction, fresh ideas, inspired words and Holy Spirit focus to live a life directed by Jesus Himself. Here you will find how to use the weapons of our warfare to prepare for battle and to understand the fog of war. There is even a chapter called "Night-Vision Goggles" that will help you detect and overcome the deception all around us.

You will be captivated by numerous examples of the warrior ethos in Bible characters such as David, Moses, Elijah, Daniel and others. Scripture references abound, giving us the foundation on which to build the army of the Lord—or, as I say, *Adonai*'s army.

I was fascinated to read an observation in the introduction that, in the military, everyone has heard a thousand times: Complacency can kill you. We need to prepare for the unexpected. Deception will keep us complacent and actually ensure our demise if we are negligent in our approach to life. Understanding the enemy's deceptive strategies is the key to gaining wisdom and defeating the devil. Giammona and Anderson show us with real-life and personal inspirational stories, as well as written guidelines, how to become battle ready.

In recent years the Church has been dedicated to making converts, but not disciples trained to avoid the pitfalls of deception and ready for spiritual combat.

This book is the training manual for the coming revival and revolution of the Church. Many today are talking of revival. My concern is what happens after the revival ends. This book answers the question "Then what?"

Join us in the worldwide revolution of the Church that, in these end times, will fight the powers of darkness, win the many and enlist disciples as warriors for our Messiah.

Dr. Robert Jeffress, senior pastor, First Baptist Church, Dallas, Texas; adjunct professor, Dallas Theological Seminary; television host, *Pathway to Victory*

Preface

Did God Really Say?

"Did God really say?" is the refrain echoed throughout the centuries of humankind's war with the forces of darkness. That question—originally posed by Satan to Eve in the Garden of Eden (see Genesis 3:1), resulting in the Fall of humankind—is the mantra of a world now hurtling toward the end at a breathtaking pace.

Doubting God's Word and His very existence is the norm in our culture, and that drumbeat will continue and grow until Jesus Christ returns and extinguishes deception and replaces it with the truth of His Kingdom.

The purpose of this book is to train people of all ages to fight and overcome deception by standing firm in their faith, and then to advance against the gates of hell (see Matthew 16:18). We want to rightly navigate the passageways of this world fraught with deception so we will end up in that Kingdom that will never end. And we want no one to perish because they were deceived by our culture, this world and this present darkness.

Military leaders throughout history have used the strategy of deception to win wars. It is no different today. In his end-times fight leading the forces of darkness, Satan employs advanced tactics in the realm of deception "to deceive, if possible, even the elect" (Matthew 24:24).

In this book, the sequel to our national bestseller *The Military Guide to Armageddon*, we will show you and your family how to apply military and spiritual intelligence principles in everyday life to become the soldiers of God you were destined to be.

Acknowledgments

Thank you to the phenomenal Battle Ready Ministries Board of Advisors: Troy Anderson, Irene Anderson, Pastor Coco Perez, Colonel Scott McChrystal, Jim Ellis, Major General Bob Dees, Colonel Pete Brzezinski, Kevin Callahan, John Barker, Chris McGahan, Mary Ann Peluso McGahan and Jerry Moses.

Special thanks to Reverend Kevin Jessip, Dave Dias, Frank Wright and Pastor Sammy Rodriquez and to all those whose lives have touched me (David) spiritually in special ways.

I would be remiss if I failed to acknowledge all who have served, are serving and will serve in our magnificent United States armed forces around the world, with whom I have had the privilege to serve alongside through many dangers, toils and snares.

We would further like to thank those who graciously took time to do interviews for the book, including Rabbi Jonathan Bernis, Dr. Robert Jeffress, Pastor Jimmy Evans, Reverend Jessip, Colonel Brzezinski, Dr. Paul McGuire, Rabbi Jonathan Cahn,

Peluso McGahan, Alex Newman, Dr. Hugh Ross, Lucas Miles, Pastor Greg Laurie, Jerry Moses and Pastor Paul Pickern.

I (Troy) would like to thank our Bible study group, led by David and Esther, who have prayed for the Lord's guidance and blessing over this project and others for a decade; our Film Prayer Warriors team, who prayed for spiritual covering over *The Military Guide to Disarming Deception*; and Jerry Moses, for his wisdom, prayers and belief in this project.

We would also like to thank our incredible literary agent, Bryan Norman, president of Alive Literary Agency, for his encouragement and belief in this series of books.

In addition, we would like to thank David Sluka, Jane Campbell and the entire team at Chosen Books for their confidence in how the Lord plans to use *The Military Guide to Disarming Deception*.

Finally, we would like to thank everyone who endorsed the book or was a part of the launch teams to help us get the word out to readers. May the Holy Spirit use this book to disarm the deception increasingly abroad in our world, as the end draws nearer.

PART 1

SPIRITUAL DECEPTION

1

Complacency Can Kill You

"Watch out that no one deceives you."

MATTHEW 24:4

SUMMER 1991
KHOBAR TOWERS, BUILDING 131, DHAHRAN, SAUDI ARABIA
EARLY MORNING

"Sir, I am concerned about the safety and welfare of our troops in this location," I told my commander.

"What do you mean, Chaplain?"

"I mean that this building that houses our troops is so close to the road and vulnerable to enemy attack," I answered.

That commander probably thought, *Hey, what do you know? You're just a chaplain, and I'm a hardened infantry soldier with years of experience.*

He replied, "Nonsense, Chaplain. We've spent a lot of time hardening this site and have taken all necessary precautions."

"Very well, sir," I replied.

But I was not convinced.

SUMMER 1996

It shook me to my core. In Rose Barracks, Germany, I could not believe what I was reading, yet I had predicted the outcome five years before: Nineteen airmen had died and more than four hundred U.S. and international military members and civilians had been injured in the terrorist attack at Khobar Towers in Dhahran, Saudi Arabia, on June 25, 1996.

The front of Building 131 was blown off, exposing eight stories of rooms after terrorists detonated a fuel truck parked nearby. Khobar Towers had been attacked by a truck bomb, and many U.S. Air Force 4404th Wing personnel were wounded and killed in the very place I had stood.

Even military commanders can get lulled into complacency—defined as self-satisfaction, especially when accompanied by unawareness of actual dangers or deficiencies—when everything is going well. Our enemies, however, whether spiritual or physical, never rest. Encouraging complacency is one of the major components of deception.

Deception has played a major role in history, especially in the military. When I attended the U.S. Army War College, Chinese general, writer and philosopher Sun Tzu was referred to frequently as one of the great architects of modern warfare. One of his topics was military deception. Sun Tzu's greatest work, *The Art of War*, lays out the formula for success in war.

Deception, in Sun Tzu's world, is a priority military tactic, meaning that it was at the top of his list of important methods of winning battles. His famous quote on the subject sums it up nicely: "All warfare is based on deception."[1]

Often in war, the enemy tries to lull his opponent into complacency. This is accomplished through patience and perseverance. The Taliban waited for years, for example, until the United States wanted nothing more than to end the twenty-year war in Afghanistan. In 2021 America pulled out too quickly, leaving behind tons of equipment and Afghan National Army personnel. The results were catastrophic.

The Coming of the Master Deceiver

The Bible tells us that the end times will be marked by false prophets claiming they are Christ, spreading deception. But a global dictator is coming, a master deceiver and a patient diplomat with incredible negotiating skills—a figure known as the Antichrist, empowered by the devil, "a liar and the father of lies" (John 8:44)—who will preside over the deaths of half to two-thirds or more of the world's population during the seven-year Tribulation prior to the return of Jesus Christ.

The world will look to him to solve incredibly complex economic, political and military problems. He will use mesmerizing oratorical and other skills to lull the world into believing that it will enjoy peace and prosperity under his rule. He will be a smooth operator who wins the masses with his cunning, skill and miracle-working powers.

The Bible warns that the Antichrist will deceive people, who will believe "the lie." The apostle Paul talks about this "lie": God will send "a powerful delusion so that they will believe the lie" (2 Thessalonians 2:11). The lie they will believe is the claim of this false messiah, the Antichrist. And this lie goes back to the Garden of Eden when Satan said to Adam and Eve, "Did God really say?" Lucifer questioned and then contradicted what God had told them. Genesis 3:1–5 tells the story:

> The serpent was more crafty than any of the wild animals the LORD God had made. He said to the woman, "Did God really say, 'You must not eat from any tree in the garden'?" The woman said to the serpent, "We may eat fruit from the trees in the garden, but God did say, 'You must not eat fruit from the tree that is in the middle of the garden, and you must not touch

it, or you will die.'" "You will not certainly die," the serpent said to the woman. "For God knows that when you eat from it your eyes will be opened, and you will be like God, knowing good and evil."

Greg Laurie, senior pastor of the fifteen-thousand-member Harvest Christian Fellowship in Riverside, California, and founder of Harvest Crusades and Harvest America, explains how Bible-believing, well-taught Christians will avoid believing the lie in the end times:

> The only way we're going to recognize an error is by knowing the truth. I was speaking with a friend who worked for the police department in the counterfeit division, and he told me that they never handle counterfeit money. They only handle real currency, so when they touch the counterfeit, they immediately know.
>
> It's a temptation not to believe the Word of God as a source of authority, but to believe something else in its place. That's the "lie." We don't want that to happen to us. We need to think biblically; we need to live biblically. I think when you're immersed in Scripture, you have everything you need. You have the moral compass you need. You have the clear sense of right and wrong. Everything you need to know about God is found in the Bible. And I think everything you need to know about life is also found in the Bible.[2]

In His first act of public ministry, which He intended as a sign to Israel that He was the Messiah, Jesus defied the religious leaders of His day, chastising them for commercializing and trivializing the house of God. After He overturned the tables of the money changers and drove them out of the Temple, saying they had turned "My Father's house" into a "house of merchandise" (John 2:16 NKJV), the gospel writer pointed out the innate sinful nature of humankind:

26

When He was in Jerusalem at the Passover, during the feast, many believed in His name when they saw the signs which He did. But Jesus did not commit Himself to them, because He knew all men, and had no need that anyone should testify of man, for He knew what was in man.

John 2:23–25 NKJV

Jesus' response to deception and the human condition lay at the core of His relationship to the crowds that followed Him.

Standing Firm against Lies and Deception

Today we must stand firm against the lies and deception of the enemy with the unshakable knowledge of Jesus and the truth of the Gospel. To begin with, we must learn what deception is, what snares the enemy is laying for us and how we can overcome "the trap of the devil" (2 Timothy 2:26).

In every battle in every war in history, leaders and their followers prepared for war by studying the schemes, plans and strategies of the enemy, to try to be victorious. It is the same for followers of Jesus.

Deception has been perpetrated since the beginning of time, but the Bible indicates that deception will increase until Christ comes:

The coming of the lawless one will be in accordance with how Satan works. He will use all sorts of displays of power through signs and wonders that serve the lie, and all the ways that wickedness deceives those who are perishing. They perish because they refused to love the truth and so be saved. For this reason God sends them a powerful delusion so that they will believe the lie and so that all will be condemned who have not believed the truth but have delighted in wickedness.

2 Thessalonians 2:9–12

When Jesus told His disciples about the coming destruction of the Temple, He also warned them, and us, against deception:

> "Truly I tell you, not one stone here will be left on another; every one will be thrown down." . . . "Tell us," they said, "when will this happen, and what will be the sign of your coming and of the end of the age?" Jesus answered: "Watch out that no one deceives you."
>
> Matthew 24:2–4

His prediction must have thrown them into a tailspin. "What do You mean that these magnificent buildings will be destroyed? That's not possible. We've been visiting this magnificent Temple all our lives. We are comfortable here. Things cannot be as bad as You say."

Do not get complacent! In the military everyone has heard it a thousand times: "Complacency can kill you." Instead, we need to prepare for the inevitable. The day-to-day grind of everyday events, the onslaught of news and the constant drone of social media can lull us into a false sense of security. But complacency, as I said, is one of the major components of deception in the end times; and if we are negligent in our approach to life, deception will keep us complacent, lead us astray and ensure our demise.

Understanding the enemy's deceptive strategies, then, is key to gaining wisdom and defeating the devil.

"There is nothing more important than this topic for a Christian," says Paul McGuire, an internationally recognized prophecy expert; commentator on CNN, Fox News and the History Channel; and former host of the nationally syndicated *Paul McGuire Show*. "The Bible teaches us that every satanic system shares one thing in common: They all move forward through the use of either spiritual deception or psychological deception."[3]

The devil employs and energizes many different ideologies, religions and belief systems to lull us into complacency and spread deception so that we will not come to a saving knowledge of Christ or awaken to the reality that powerful forces are setting the global stage for the rise of the Antichrist.

This book is designed not only to alert you to the signs of the end times, but to help you avoid the pitfalls of deception enveloping the planet today. It will help you walk in the supernatural power, protection and provision of the Holy Spirit amid the pervasive deception arising in these last days. Our overarching goal is to inform, enlighten and prepare you to navigate the propaganda, disinformation and deceptive ideologies that have infiltrated the Church and society.

Each chapter of this book looks at deception through the lens of the end times, the Bible, the military and current events. It uses a personal anecdote related to deception, a U.S. Army term or technique and spiritual warfare disciplines and strategies to help you become a battle-ready warrior of God prepared for "the glorious appearing" of Jesus Christ (Titus 2:13 NKJV).

We will explore ways of ensuring that you and your loved ones are prepared for the continuous onslaught of false information, propaganda, diabolical doctrines and a host of other deceitful tactics of the enemy.

TACTICS, TECHNIQUES AND PROCEDURES

At the end of every chapter, we will suggest tactics, techniques and procedures based on military principles that will transform your life as you practice and apply them. Here are some to get you started:

1. **Reach for spiritual growth.** What is one area in which you would like to grow? Ask the Holy Spirit and reach out to a trusted person to get his or her advice on how to improve in this area.

2. **Do not settle.** Have a continual improvement attitude. In other words, do not settle for where you are in your relationship with the Lord. "Without faith it is impossible to please God, for he who comes to God must believe that He exists and that He is a rewarder of those who diligently seek Him" (Hebrews 11:6 MEV).

3. **Change things up.** It is difficult to do the same thing every day without an end in sight. Change a common routine you have in some way—shift focus—so you can take time for yourself, your family and your relationship with God. The military uses forced change to refocus the troops and alleviate complacency.

4. **Schedule devotional time.** Set up a time to gather your family or close friends for a devotional or Bible reading time when you impart God's Word to yourself and your loved ones. Know that as you read and speak God's Word, that Word will be imparted to you. If possible, schedule a regular time to do this.

5. **Learn from mistakes (AAR).** The military uses After Action Reviews to highlight what went right and to learn from mistakes. What sin or mistake are you tired of repeating? Ask the Holy Spirit to show you a fresh approach—something you have not done before. Do not let your past dictate your future.

2

The Great Rebellion

Don't let anyone deceive you in any way, for that day will not
come until the rebellion occurs and the man of lawlessness is
revealed, the man doomed to destruction.

2 THESSALONIANS 2:3

EARLY 1990S
COMBAT MANEUVER TRAINING CENTER (CMTC)
HOHENFELS, GERMANY

We were in the "box," and my heavy tank unit was training to
go to war. The U.S. Army prepared us by placing units in real-
istic force-on-force training scenarios amid the rugged terrain
of the CMTC. I witnessed weather there that I have not seen
anywhere else. In one day you could see snow, rain, wind, fog,
sunshine, cold, heat—you name it.

I was in my High Mobility Multipurpose Wheeled Vehicle
(Humvee) with my assistant driving behind our task force Sergeant Major. He was leading the way into the "box," and we

31

were right behind him, when suddenly he came to a complete stop and got out of his vehicle. I joined him to survey a large and rather deep water-filled mud puddle right in the middle of the road, blocking our way.

"What do you think, Sergeant Major?" I asked. "Do you want to chance going through that?"

He replied brashly, "Chaplain, I've been in the Army for over twenty years. This little thing ain't going to stop me."

"It's your call, Sergeant Major," I replied.

He got back in that armored Humvee and told the driver to step on it. Sure as shooting, that Humvee drove forward right into the middle of that mudhole and sank all the way down to the axles.

Sergeant Major's face was red as a beet. I suppressed my laughter. But it was one heck of sight to see the task force Sergeant Major stuck in the middle of that mudhole. He looked over at me as if to say, "Chaplain, don't even say it," then called for an M113 armored personnel carrier to pull him out with its heavy chain.

I learned an important lesson that day. The mud puddle in front of us may have looked passable, at least to him, but it was not. Looks were deceptive. Instead of using the proper TTPs (Tactics, Techniques and Procedures), Sergeant Major decided to forge ahead on his own, and he paid the price.

Pride and arrogance will defeat you every time. Also, just because something in front of you looks good does not mean it is good, especially when others are warning you off.

One of the Enemy's Greatest Weapons

In one of the greatest deceptions in the history of warfare, Operation Fortitude in World War II, the Allies under General Dwight D. Eisenhower deployed a totally fake army under the command of the most feared general of the war, George S.

Patton. The Germans considered Patton as the Allies' greatest leader and never for a moment thought he would be used as part of a deceptive strategy. But that is exactly what happened.

Patton was placed in charge of a fictitious army on the coast of England preparing for an "invasion" focused on Calais, France, while the real invasion was to take place at Normandy. The reason for the success of Operation Overlord, the invasion of Europe through Normandy, was in part due to the deceptive tactics of the Allies.

"One of the key things I learned in the military," says retired U.S. Army Chaplain (Col.) Peter Brzezinski, "is that deception is definitely a means to multiply your strength. If I can get you to pay attention to this area over here in your blind spot, I can come at you from another direction with the main effort." He uses the Gulf War in 1991 in Kuwait as an example.

> General Norman Schwarzkopf basically did that with the Kuwaitis. He made it look like the attack was going to be an amphibious landing through Kuwait with the Marines, so they had enough forces out there to distract the Iraqis, when the main event was to come up through the desert on a flanking maneuver. The enemy does the same thing. He gives us just enough distraction to make it look real on something he's doing, but he's distracting you so he can attack you with the main effort from another direction.[1]

There have been numerous conflicts, and with them, deceptive tactics, before and after World War II. Here is where rebellion—the subject of this chapter—comes in. Along with the deception proliferating worldwide, the world is rebelling against God and God-given conscience by trying to normalize sin. What used to be black or white is now gray. Rebellion against God and His principles is snowballing. Human beings think they know better than God how to live in this world. My

Sergeant Major in Hohenfels, Germany, thought he knew best, and found himself sinking in the quagmire as a result.

Just when we think we know something through years of experience, assumptions can lead us to disaster. Deception is that way. What looks good and right is not always what it seems. Unless we are grounded in the Word of God, we can easily be misled by the pressures of our culture, especially in today's "cancel culture"—"canceling" or ostracizing those who say or do something not socially accepted. "Cancel culture" is a tactic that progressive activists use, in the words of Charles Snow, "to silence those who say things or hold positions with which they disagree."[2]

Another movement in recent years is "wokeism"—being alert to issues of racial and social justice. God is the creator and source of justice, and He hates injustice and oppression. Scripture declares in several places that "righteousness and justice are the foundation of [God's] throne" (Psalm 89:14; see also Psalm 97:2, Proverbs 16:12). But the movements of cancel culture and wokeism, which started in an attempt to stop racism and social injustice, now seek to silence those who disagree with their progressive ideas.

Both movements have their roots in Germany in 1923 with the establishment of the Institute for Social Research (ISR), currently part of Goethe University Frankfurt in Germany. The ISR was founded by Felix Weil, a student of the Marxist philosopher Karl Korsch, and led by other Marxist thinkers trained by Russia's secret police to ignite Marxist revolutions in Western nations. The so-called Frankfurt School Marxists came to the U.S. in 1934 and became affiliated with Columbia University in New York City. They obtained positions as professors at other Ivy League universities as well. Their goal: to start a socialist revolution in the U.S. and other Western nations but conceal it under the guise of a cultural revolution.[3]

Nationally syndicated talk radio host Mark R. Levin, with a J.D. from Temple University School of Law, recognizes the Marxist roots of wokeism. He explains that woke activists

> use the tactics of propaganda and indoctrination, and demand conformity and compliance, silencing contrary voices through repressive tactics, such as "cancel culture," which destroys reputations and careers, censoring and banning most patriotic and contrary viewpoints on social media . . . , and attacking academic freedom and intellectual interchange in higher education.
>
> What is occurring in our country is not a temporary fad or passing event. American Marxism exists, it is pervasive, and its multitude of hybrid but often interlocking movements are actively working to destroy our society and culture and overthrow the country as we know it.[4]

Paul McGuire, Bible prophecy expert and news commentator, offers these insights:

> The key strategies of the Frankfurt School Marxists reveal the satanic nature of their deception and operation. Their number one goal was to destroy Christianity. Their number two goal was the destruction of the family unit. Their number three goal was to destroy any sense of biblical right or wrong. And their fourth goal was to destroy any concept of patriotism.
>
> They were motivated by the spirit of Antichrist. They are still operational today, spreading their deception. Christians will never defeat Communism and Marxism until they understand that they are nothing more than a Trojan horse for Satanism.[5]

Rebelling against Truth

The verse quoted at the beginning of this chapter is critically important in our understanding of deception and rebellion in the end times:

Don't let anyone deceive you in any way, for that day will not come until the rebellion occurs and the man of lawlessness is revealed, the man doomed to destruction.

2 Thessalonians 2:3

Troy and I have believed for years that this rebellion would be led by unbelievers. And many unbelievers have indeed paved the way, as we have just noted, in rebellion against God. But upon further study and research, Troy and I now think this rebellion is by believers.

The word for *rebellion* in the Greek is *apostasia*—meaning apostasy, falling away, defection. The question is, falling away from what? When the apostle Paul wrote that warning, he was addressing a problem in the Thessalonian church—a teaching running rampant that Christ had already returned; so Paul was telling them not to panic or lose their minds. Jesus could not come back, he wrote, until two things happened: "the rebellion" and the revelation of the man of lawlessness, the Antichrist. The context makes it clear: Paul is warning believers not to fall away from their faith.

Jesus addressed the same issue of false teaching in Matthew 24:10–11: "At that time many will turn away from the faith and will betray and hate each other, and many false prophets will appear and deceive many people."

At what time? The end of time, or just before the return of Christ in the *parousia*, or Second Coming.

The Mark of the Beast

What would cause millions of believers around the world to abandon their faith and rebel against the truth? The book of Revelation answers that question:

Then I saw a second beast, coming out of the earth. It had two horns like a lamb, but it spoke like a dragon. It exercised all the authority of the first beast on its behalf, and made the earth and its inhabitants worship the first beast, whose fatal wound had been healed. And it performed great signs, even causing fire to come down from heaven to the earth in full view of the people. Because of the signs it was given power to perform on behalf of the first beast, it deceived the inhabitants of the earth. . . . It also forced all people, great and small, rich and poor, free and slave, to receive a mark on their right hands or on their foreheads, so that they could not buy or sell unless they had the mark, which is the name of the beast or the number of its name.

Revelation 13:11–14, 16–17

For the first time in history, the technologies exist—artificial intelligence, electronic banking, digital currency, microchips, neural implants, digital tattoos, nanorobotics technologies, the surveillance state and more—for a "mark of the Beast" system to be put into place without which people could not "buy or sell."

Jimmy Evans, founder and president of XO Marriage, former senior pastor at Trinity Fellowship Church in Amarillo, Texas, and host, along with his wife, Karen, of the nationally syndicated television show *Marriage Today with Jimmy & Karen*, expands on what the mark of the Beast will signify:

> The mark of the Beast is a mark of allegiance to the beliefs of the Antichrist system, which completely rejects the Word of God and the deity of Jesus Christ. *Anti* means two things: It means "against" and it means "instead of." The Antichrist is also called "the lawless one." The word *lawless* is *anomia* in the Greek, meaning "against law." He is anti-Word. And now he comes and says, "You will believe this. You will practice this. You will not do this. If you agree, take the mark. And if you take the mark, you can be employed. You can travel. You can transact business. If you do not take the mark, you're completely outcast from society and you'll pay the price."

I'm sure there will be an underground market during the Tribulation, some way to get goods and services from fellow Christians, but it's going to be a tough time, and people will be martyred and beheaded for their faith in Christ and for not taking the mark.[6]

Receiving the Mark

Many have written about Revelation 13:11–17, with different ideas on how to look at it. From our perspective there are five key things that stand out:

1. This mark is not going to sneak up on humanity in the middle of the night; it will be forced upon humankind for all to see. And with that, all who take it will worship the Beast, much as in the first century, when Christians were forced to acknowledge the Roman emperor as lord and God. Toward the end of the first century, the emperor Domitian issued a decree that all in his empire should worship him as "God the Lord." Citizens were ordered to come to the public square, burn a pinch of incense and say, "*Caesar kurios*," meaning "Caesar is lord." Christians who refused were imprisoned and executed.[7]
2. Refusal to take the mark will end in death. Those who somehow escape will be forced into hiding and will deal somehow in the underground economy to survive.
3. It will be worldwide. Although some scholars believe it to be biblical hyperbole and limited to the Middle East and the ten-nation confederacy, we believe it will be required globally, since the Bible clearly indicates this: "All inhabitants of the earth will worship the beast—all whose names have not been written in the Lamb's book of life" (Revelation 13:8).
4. The mark will be some kind of digital implant or mark for which the technology to implement already exists. There are many conjectures out there saying that this or that is

the mark of the Beast. But remember, to take the mark, you must swear allegiance and worship the Beast publicly as Lord and God. Once you do, there is no repentance, according to the Bible (see Revelation 14:9–11).

5. Those will be very difficult times. People will have to choose between life or death, Christ or Satan, safety (for a season) or persecution. Now, then, is the time to get right with God, prepare your faith and consider the eternal consequences of taking the mark. There is no avoiding the decision, as it will affect all who are around you, as well as your own eternal destiny.

Believing the Lie

The Word of God tells us that the second Beast mentioned in Revelation 13, called by some scholars the false prophet, will perform miraculous signs, such as commanding fire to fall out of heaven to earth. Many believers, Jesus warned, will follow that man who proclaims himself to be God and demonstrates it by powerful, miraculous signs:

"At that time if anyone says to you, 'Look, here is the Messiah!' or, 'There he is!' do not believe it. For false messiahs and false prophets will appear and perform great signs and wonders to deceive, if possible, even the elect. See, I have told you ahead of time. So if anyone tells you, 'There he is, out in the wilderness,' do not go out; or, 'Here he is, in the inner rooms,' do not believe it. For as lightning that comes from the east is visible even in the west, so will be the coming of the Son of Man."

Matthew 24:22–27

Please pay attention to this. It may be the most important thing you will decide in your lifetime. The return of Jesus Christ will not be in some hidden back street or underground tunnel; it will be in full view of the entire planet. Although millions will be deceived, you do not have to be one of them. People will be deceived only because they rebelled against the truth of Jesus' words.

The apostle Paul identified the forms this rebellion will take:

> But mark this: There will be terrible times in the last days. People will be lovers of themselves, lovers of money, boastful, proud, abusive, disobedient to their parents, ungrateful, unholy, without love, unforgiving, slanderous, without self-control, brutal, not lovers of the good, treacherous, rash, conceited, lovers of pleasure rather than lovers of God— having a form of godliness but denying its power. Have nothing to do with such people.
>
> 2 Timothy 3:1–5

This passage is key to understanding the end times. Many, including those who attend church or purport to believe in God, will be caught up in the end-times rebellion because of the lawlessness abounding. The "powerful delusion" Paul refers to in 2 Thessalonians 2:11 is sent by God because people refuse to believe the truth of the Gospel. So instead, they believe the lie.

Dr. Robert Jeffress, senior pastor of the thirteen-thousand-member First Baptist Church in Dallas, Texas, and adjunct professor at Dallas Theological Seminary, calls Satan a "nonpartisan liar," pointing to Jesus' characterization of him in John 8:44 as "a liar and the father of lies." Jeffress, host of the *Pathway to Victory* television show broadcast globally, agrees that the "powerful delusion" refers to the Antichrist himself under the control of Satan:

> But I think the theological delusion we will see manifest in the Antichrist is very pervasive in the world right now. I call it the way of Cain in the Bible. The Bible tells us to avoid the way of Cain. What in the world is the way of Cain? God invited

both of the two brothers, Cain and Abel, to come to Him on His terms, but Cain decided he had a better way to approach God—on his own terms with his own sacrifice. Since that time man has tried to approach God in his own way.

Jesus said in John 14:6: "I am the way and the truth and the life. No one comes to the Father except through me." One of the most distressing things to me as a pastor is that nearly sixty percent of evangelical Christians believe there is more than one way to God other than faith in Jesus Christ. That's a delusion we are experiencing right now that will only increase during the times of the Antichrist.[8]

Rebellion on the Rise

Rebellion and deception have always been part of the war against God and His saints. This rebellion in our society today includes false doctrines, propaganda, disinformation, political agendas, misleading news, revisionist history, deceptive ideologies, arrogant lies and made-up facts, all of which contribute to a planet deluged with deception.

Deception has been with us since the beginning. Will it be with us when Jesus returns and beyond? Yes, even at the end of the Millennium, when Jesus has reigned for a thousand years:

> When the thousand years are over, Satan will be released from his prison and will go out to deceive the nations in the four corners of the earth—Gog and Magog—and to gather them for battle. In number they are like the sand on the seashore. They marched across the breadth of the earth and surrounded the camp of God's people, the city he loves. But fire came down from heaven and devoured them. And the devil, who deceived them, was thrown into the lake of burning sulfur, where the beast and the false prophet had been thrown. They will be tormented day and night for ever and ever.
>
> Revelation 20:7–10

Since deception in these last days is running rampant, finding its way into every area of our lives, it is vitally important that we recognize deception and its ramifications during these perilous times.

New York Times bestselling author Rabbi Jonathan Cahn says we are in a time of "great shakings." Cahn, the senior rabbi at the Beth Israel Jerusalem Center in Wayne, New Jersey, says that "the purpose of these events is for God calling His people back to Him and for revival."[9]

Cahn is not alone. Many faith leaders also believe that the world is at a critical juncture in history.

"We're in a much more advanced state of apostasy," says Cahn. "We are seeing things in our culture most people would never have dreamed of. We are being shaken to our core." He believes America is replaying an ancient judgment mystery that also happened in the last days of ancient Israel.

> All the signs have reappeared, and we are now progressing toward it. But the template is that we've got a window of time. The Lord gives a nation a window of time to come back to Him—either to repent and go toward revival, or to go away from God and head to judgment. We have increasing signs that the window is coming to a close, and if we don't come back to God, we head to judgment, so this is crucial. Revival is not just a nice thing. It is life and death.[10]

The Bible says that the false teachers in Paul's day who were promoting rebellion and deception were servants of Satan himself:

> Such people are false apostles, deceitful workers, masquerading as apostles of Christ. And no wonder, for Satan himself masquerades as an angel of light. It is not surprising, then, if his servants also masquerade as servants of righteousness. Their end will be what their actions deserve.
>
> 2 Corinthians 11:13–15

Today the world says, "I can't serve a God who doesn't address our cultural sensitivities." It wants a weak God who is culturally sensitive and permissive, a God who allows us to do and believe whatever we want.

But this is rebellion. Thus, while 51 percent of American adults claim to have a biblical worldview, according to evangelical pollster George Barna, only 6 percent actually hold such a worldview. Of that 51 percent, for example, 49 percent say reincarnation is a possibility after they die. And only 33 percent say they believe that "human beings are born with a sinful nature and can only be saved from the consequences of sin by Jesus Christ."[11]

So we have turned away from biblical teaching, as in the book of Judges, when the ancient Israelites rebelled against the Law and the ways of Moses and Joshua, when "everyone did what was right in his own eyes" (Judges 17:6; 21:25 NKJV).

Many Western, so-called Christian nations could mostly count on the consistency of its people's faith commitments. But over the past three decades, the dramatic erosion of shared Christian beliefs has ushered in many radical changes in religious alignments. Barna found 34 percent of people—and 43 percent of young people—saying they "don't know, don't care, or don't believe that God exists," a nearly threefold increase in recent decades.[12]

One of the most surprising revelations in Barna's research is the renewed interest in reincarnation. After Americans flirted with that belief in the psychedelic 1970s, reincarnation barely registered as an eternal outcome in polls throughout the 1990s and into the new Millennium. The last decade, however, has ignited a new following for Eastern religious thought and practices, so that today more than half of people in their twenties and thirties, and 36 percent of self-identified Christians, believe reincarnation is a possibility for them after they die, while just 2 percent of Americans believe they will experience hell when they die. Barna calls this growing group "technologically advanced, sexually unrestrained, emotionally unpredictable, and a spiritual hybrid."[13]

Satan paints the picture, one that is embraced widely today, of a weak, anemic Jesus who would not hurt a fly and loves everyone. He is indeed full of love and compassion—the reason He came to die on the cross on our behalf. But He is also Lord of lords and King of kings, and He will come to destroy rebellion and rule this planet with a rod of iron (see Revelation 2:27).

TACTICS, TECHNIQUES AND PROCEDURES

Just as the military has TTPs for almost any situation in combat, the Bible gives us the tools to disarm deception in our lives and the lives of our loved ones:

1. **"Do not believe every spirit"** (1 John 4:1). There are many false prophets, animated by deceitful spirits. The world is chaotic because Satan is the author of confusion. Be careful not to fall for every prophetic word, dream, vision or other such revelation. We must test all messages purported to be from God by the gold standard, His Word. What in the past did you believe but later realized was not true? What changed? How did you uncover the truth? Ask the Lord for wisdom and to sharpen your sense to discern what is right.

2. **Test truth.** "Do not despise prophecies. Test all things; hold fast what is good" (1 Thessalonians 5:20–21 NKJV). Our culture, politicians, government, educators and influencers do not get to decide truth. God does. Evaluate

the messages of our culture by using the Bible as the standard or rule of measure. Is it okay, for example, to tell a lie under certain circumstances? According to Proverbs 12:22, "The LORD detests lying lips, but he delights in people who are trustworthy."

3. **Understand changing language.** *Euphemism* is substituting a word considered unpleasant or offensive with a softer word. Instead of saying that a person died, we say that he or she passed away. Instead of being unemployed, we say that a person is now "between jobs." Can you think of one phrase used in the past that means something different today? Learn to decipher words and their meanings. Over time, words we thought we knew have changed. People today talk about "my truth," as if it is different from "your truth," as if truth is relative, and if you simply believe something to be true, then it is. Hundreds of words and phrases are used today that meant something different in the past. "I send you out as sheep in the midst of wolves," said Jesus. "Be wise as serpents and harmless as doves" (Matthew 10:16 NJKV).

4. **Walk in the Word.** Since the Word of God is the gold standard for every believer, exercise your authority as a believer and gain insight and understanding into God's Word. Ask the Holy Spirit for a passage of Scripture each day. Read it, say it out loud and put it into practice, to become a "doer" of the Word (see James 1:22–25).

3

Subversion

The supreme art of war is to subdue the enemy without fighting.

SUN TZU

LATE 2005
AFGHANISTAN, OUTSIDE THE WIRE OF BAGRAM AIRFIELD
NEAR PARWAN PROVINCE

I am riding in an armed convoy bringing clothing and goods to some of the tribes. It is what the Army calls a "Hearts and Minds" mission. We want the people of the region to understand that we are not here to kill them, but to help win their friendship by supplying much-needed clothing. But it feels surreal because on the way to the tribes, we see signs along the way with a skull and crossbones and the words *Mines! Do Not Get Off the Road!*

What I witness is heartbreaking—children running around barefoot in this cold, mountainous region. The elders of the tribe greet us warmly, and the people of the tribe appear glad we came. The exchange goes off without a hitch. We are in a battle for the hearts and minds of the people of Afghanistan, but on this day, at least, I believe we have helped the tribe.

The Taliban and other insurgents throughout Afghanistan use nonmilitary tactics against the people. Their weapons of choice are most often fear and reprisal. If they discover Afghans working with the United States coalition, those people and their families might end up dead. The insurgents continue to hunt down those not aligned with their views, including Christians and Western workers.

Not all warfare, then, involves the use of military weapons to defeat the enemy. There are other ways of conducting war.

The use of diplomatic, informational, military and economic tools (DIME) as a means of influence has been a weapon in the U.S. arsenal for years. The DIME acronym is part of how "nations use the power available to them to exercise control over people, places, things, and events to achieve objectives in accordance with their national interests and policies."[1]

What does this mean, exactly? It means that national interests can be advanced through nonmilitary means. In the case of distributing clothing and goods to tribes in Afghanistan, both diplomacy and economics were used (two of the letters in DIME). There are other uses of national power as well. But for the purposes of this book, we will keep it simple and use the DIME paradigm.

All around the world today, especially in China and Russia, the use of nonmilitary power is evident. Those two nations are using their vast economic resources to build infrastructure in Africa and Asia to bring their brand of influence to those parts of the world. Even with trade agreements in place, how many products around the globe are still "Made in China"?

One of the uses of national power that is primarily non-military is subversion. According to the U.S. Department of

Defense, subversion includes "actions designed to undermine the military, economic, psychological, or political strength or morale of a governing authority."[2] Under that definition, subversion is a means of military, economic, psychological and political warfare.

National security professional J. Michael Waller writes that subversion is an "ambiguous form of conflict in war and peace that does not rely on violence . . . so ambiguous—and often gradual and long-term—that American diplomatic, security, and military planners find it difficult to identify, recognize, understand, and neutralize." Subversion is also "the undermining or detachment of the loyalties of significant political and social groups within the victimized state, and their transference . . . to the symbols and institutions of the aggressor."[3]

We are watching this happen today as the world and many of its leaders increasingly embrace the ideologies—Marxism, socialism and Communism—of those who have engaged in a long-term campaign of subversion in order to undermine democratic military, political, economic, religious and moral strength.

Just as in the last chapter we saw deception and rebellion going hand in hand, so deception and subversion complement and support one another. The enemy of our souls, Satan, is pulling out all the stops in his war against God and humankind; and two of his primary tactics are subverting the image and the doctrines of the Triune God.

God's Image Distorted

Satan loves making people believe that God does not exist or that He is a kindly, benevolent and nonjudgmental grandfather. (We noted in the last chapter that God is indeed kind and good, but He is also humankind's Judge, and those who do not acknowledge His Son as Lord will be separated from Him forever.) The enemy has inspired religions with a variety of images other than the one, true, almighty, all-powerful, all-knowing, all-loving God described in Psalm 139 and throughout the Bible.

Satan distorts Jesus, the Son of God, to be a good teacher, an example of love to follow—a prophet or higher spiritual being, even—but not the coequal Second Person of the Trinity. Do you recognize the source of these lies? Listen to the apostle John:

> Every spirit that does not acknowledge Jesus is not from God. This is the spirit of the antichrist, which you have heard is coming and even now is already in the world.
>
> 1 John 4:3

The Barna Group, in research about what Americans believe about Jesus, finds that although many say they believe in Him, they do not understand who He is. Millennials, for example, "are the only generation among whom fewer than half believe Jesus was God (48 percent). About one-third of young adults (35 percent) say instead that Jesus was merely a religious or spiritual leader, while 17 percent aren't sure what he was."[4]

In chapter 1 we read Jesus' prophecy that "false christs and false prophets will arise and perform great signs and wonders, so as to lead astray, if possible, even the elect" (Matthew 24:24 ESV). Many of us interpret this to mean that those will come who claim to be Christ Himself and mislead many. This is true. But there is, we believe, a broader meaning to this passage—that many will come in the last days with deceptive words and power to mislead many about the Person and work of Jesus Christ. This is happening!

A third tactic of Satan is to subvert our belief in the Holy Spirit as the Third Person of the Trinity. Jesus described Him as "the Helper [who] will teach you all things, and bring to your remembrance all things that I said to you" (John 14:26 NKJV). And just before ascending to heaven, Jesus told His disciples,

> "You will receive power when the Holy Spirit comes on you; and you will be my witnesses in Jerusalem, and in all Judea and Samaria, and to the ends of the earth."
>
> Acts 1:8

But Satan has distorted the image of the Holy Spirit to be ghostly (the King James Version translated *pneuma* as "Holy Ghost"), otherworldly, impersonal, scary, an "it" rather than a "Him," whose work is subjective, unreliable, even dangerous. We are warned not to be taken in.

#LoveWins?

Besides subverting the image of the Triune God, the enemy loves to subvert God's truth as revealed in Scripture. ("Did God really say?"—as we noted in the preface.) Three key passages of Scripture describe the spiritual subversion taking place today:

> The Spirit clearly says that in later times some will abandon the faith and follow deceiving spirits and things taught by demons.
>
> 1 Timothy 4:1

> The time will come when people will not put up with sound doctrine. Instead, to suit their own desires, they will gather around them a great number of teachers to say what their itching ears want to hear. They will turn their ears away from the truth and turn aside to myths.
>
> 2 Timothy 4:3–4

Dear friends, do not believe every spirit, but test the spirits to see whether they are from God, because many false prophets have gone out into the world.

1 John 4:1

A religious leader, Rob Bell, former pastor of Mars Hill Bible Church in Grandville, Michigan, and a *New York Times* bestselling author, has played an influential role in challenging and undermining biblical beliefs, including its teaching on hell. Bell's book *Love Wins* is an up-to-date treatise on universalism, which, in its purest form, teaches that all of us, no matter how bad or good, no matter what we do or do not believe, will end up in heaven. Bell writes:

> A staggering number of people have been taught that a select few Christians will spend forever in a peaceful, joyous place called heaven, while the rest of humanity spends forever in torment and punishment in hell with no chance for anything better. It's been clearly communicated to many that this belief is a central truth of the Christian faith and to reject it is, in essence, to reject Jesus. This is misguided and toxic and ultimately subverts the contagious spread of Jesus's message of love, peace, forgiveness, and joy that our world desperately needs to hear.[5]

Eventually all people, according to Bell, will land in heaven no matter what they did or how they lived. This sounds good, hip, cool and cutting edge until you try to align it with the Bible; then it unravels. Jesus said that the way to perdition is broad, "and many enter through it," whereas the way to heaven is narrow, "and only a few find it" (see Matthew 7:13–14). But Bell says this teaching is misguided, and he is convinced that a church that does not support same-sex marriage will "continue to be even more irrelevant."[6]

Fast-forward three years to June 2015, when the U.S. Supreme Court ruled that same-sex couples nationwide could marry. President Barack Obama tweeted, "Today is a big step in our march toward equality. Gay and lesbian couples now have the right to marry, just like anyone else. #LoveWins."[7]

Obama did not invent the "Love Wins" slogan. He got it from megachurch pastor Bell. That quote lit up the president's Twitter account, in which he was stating the predominant belief of our time: You can live however you want, and God will still accept you.

Most people now believe in many paths to God. The key is that you fulfill yourself, follow your own rules and find your own path and purpose in life.

This unprecedented deception, in defiance of God's Word, has resulted in a downward slide to depravity. What was called perverse several decades ago is now accepted by the mainstream. We are living in times when right is wrong and wrong is right—reflecting the time of the judges in Bible times (as we saw in the last chapter) when "everyone did what was right in his own eyes" (Judges 21:25 NKJV). Listen to the prophet Isaiah: "Woe to those who call evil good and good evil" (Isaiah 5:20).

Most prefer to see God as totally accepting of however they want to live, believe and view Him. They are so open-minded that they will accept just about any view of God—except the God of the Bible.

It is likely that Obama, in his #LoveWins tweet, sensed he had the support of most of the religious establishment, and that the conservative evangelical sector of the Church consisted of a bunch of out-of-touch radicals. Indeed, many Christian denominations and churches *have* traded core biblical teaching for far-left ones. There are many fallacies, falsehoods and fabrications about God in our world today being espoused not only by laypeople but also by sophisticated and trendy ministers and pastors.

It is imperative, then, that in the end times, we be aware of whom we listen to and what they believe. It is vitally important that we know and understand the Scriptures and have a true and biblical understanding. We must be aware, armed and ready to navigate the last days without falling for the subversion of truth laid out by "the god of this age" (2 Corinthians 4:4).

Vigilance for the Truth

The military is constantly vigilant for the truth. Whether it be the total number of troops in the enemy's arsenal, their strategies, tactics, types of weapons, psychological operations, etc., military leaders need the unvarnished facts.

In the same way, we as Christ-followers need to know the truth, and to develop strategies in our lives and in the lives of our loved ones to disarm the deceptive tactics of the enemy.

The Reverend Kevin Jessip, co-founder with Rabbi Jonathan Cahn of The Return: A Global Movement of Prayer and Repentance, says,

> As we begin to see biblical prophecy being fulfilled in these last days, when it lines up with real-world events, we must become aware of what's happening. We need men and women of God to stand up, like Joshua, who said, "As for me and my house, we will serve the Lord." There are things that God is calling all of us to do.[8]

Here are some things we can do every day. First, wake up each morning understanding your great need to put on the armor of God. In Paul's words,

> Stand firm then, with the belt of truth buckled around your waist, with the breastplate of righteousness in place, and with your feet fitted with the readiness that comes from the gospel

of peace. In addition to all this, take up the shield of faith, with which you can extinguish all the flaming arrows of the evil one. Take the helmet of salvation and the sword of the Spirit, which is the word of God. And pray in the Spirit on all occasions with all kinds of prayers and requests.

Ephesians 6:14–18

As you put on the full armor—including the belt of truth and the sword of the Spirit, the Word of God, to counteract the lies and subversion of the enemy—acknowledge that "this is the day the Lord has made" (Psalm 118:24 NKJV) and ask Him, "What do You want me to do today?" Then commit the day into His mighty hands.

Each day, too, be sure to repent, asking God to cleanse you from any unrighteousness, purify you and have His way with you. Jessip explains,

> God can't use a dirty vessel. I know for me, I repent daily because I'm so imperfect. There isn't a day that goes by that I can't look back and say, "I missed it again. I did something, I said something, I thought something." We must take every thought captive to the obedience of Christ. And we've got to ask for a fresh refilling of the Holy Spirit every morning. So we armor up. We ask the Holy Spirit to complete His work in us. And we ask Him to fill us so full that He can pour us out every day.[9]

TACTICS, TECHNIQUES
AND PROCEDURES

Here are four practical steps you can take to help you achieve Holy Spirit–empowered victory in your life:

1. **Be a truth-finder and -seeker.** Jesus said to ask, seek and knock (see Matthew 7:7). This applies to your strategy of knowing the truth. Always look things up in the Bible in order to understand spiritual principles and truth. Don't take a news article or somebody else's word for it. Find out for yourself by undertaking a deep and riveting study of the Word, learning the historical context of the Scriptures, consulting a solid biblical website or asking a trusted pastor. Many biblical resources are available to help you do this, including Bible handbooks.

2. **Use the weapon of truth.** "A discerning mind seeks knowledge, but the mouth of fools feeds on foolishness" (Proverbs 15:14). When reading or looking at the news, social media, magazines and other sources, look at who is behind the organization offering the information and ascertain its position or agenda. Is it left, right, socialist, Christian, atheistic? It is important to know its position to understand what it is trying to accomplish. You cannot afford to watch the news blindly without discernment.

3. **Take a life inventory, as military units do, to assess your readiness.** Take a good, hard look at your life right now: What do you believe about God, Jesus Christ and the Holy Spirit? How do your beliefs inform your life? If you really believe that Jesus is the Son of God who died for your sins, then "you were bought at a price" (1 Corinthians 6:20). Are you living under His Lordship? Jesus said if you love Him, keep His commands (see John 15:10). Remember,

giving a nod that you believe in God but continuing to live for yourself is not the pathway of following Christ.

4. **Lean on the power of the Holy Spirit.** The military uses every power it has in war. So should we! Jesus said, "All authority in heaven and on earth has been given to me" (Matthew 28:18). And He has given this authority to us: "Whoever believes in me will do the works I have been doing, and they will do even greater things than these, because I am going to the Father" (John 14:12). We have received authority over all creation from our Lord and Master, Jesus Christ. So just as Peter and John healed the lame man with a word (see Acts 3:1–8), you can see great things happen right before your eyes as you pray and speak in faith. The Lord has given you power and authority to help build His Kingdom. Use it!

4

Opposing Forces

I conceal my tracks so that none can discern them; I keep silence so that none can hear me.

SUN TZU

I am dead asleep in the back of my Humvee after a grueling training day with the storied 1st Battalion, 37th Armored Regiment (1–37 Armor). My assistant is awakened by several soldiers asking urgently for our radio-frequency codebook. They are lost, they say, and out of communication with their command, and need our codebook to transmit their location to their command, as they are late for a "commo check" (a military term that refers to verifying the transmission of critical information).

In his groggy state of mind, my sergeant hands it over to them, and they scream in glee as they run into the night with our codebook.

They have just obtained by deception a secret vital document. You see, they are the OPFOR (opposing force), and their mission that night was to obtain the secret communication codes of our armored battalion.

The next thing I know, the battalion commander sends me a message to report to our tactical operations center. He chews me out for allowing the OPFOR to take advantage of me. He was the one who sent them out that night to test all of us with our OPSEC (operational security)—our radio-frequency codebook. For it to fall into the hands of a real enemy could have devasting consequences.

I failed that night! But I learned the hard way not to let that happen ever again. And, yes, I went back to my vehicle to chew out my sergeant (everything rolls downhill in the U.S. Army!) for his failure to protect that codebook.

If this had been actual combat, that one mistake could have cost many lives. Good thing it was a training exercise to prepare us for war. Bottom line: Protect OPSEC with your very life because your life depends on it. In war, trust no one you do not know.

The military goes to great lengths to train soldiers to protect, at all costs, information that can give the enemy a distinct advantage in war. The Army uses OPFOR in training to simulate real combat situations. Part of the training is counterdeception, which "contributes to situational understanding . . . by protecting friendly command-and-control systems and decision-makers from adversary deception. Friendly decision-makers must be aware of adversary deception activities so they can formulate informed and coordinated responses."[1] These counterdeception techniques include vigilance, experience, awareness and exploitation.

What does this mean for us who are in Christ in the present world and in the last of the last days, facing the direst kind of OPFOR?

The Deception of Dark Forces

Our adversary knows his time is limited, so he is causing deception to reign throughout the world. How else can you account for mountains of false information, the flaunting of sin in the face of God, the erosion of moral and traditional values, the prevalence of misleading doctrines about God and deep divisions within the Church itself?

Let's examine his tactics in four areas in particular.

About Media

It is interesting to note that "the god of this age" (2 Corinthians 4:4) is also called "the prince of the power of the air" (Ephesians 2:2 NKJV). We believe that this powerful enemy of God has set up headquarters in strategic places around the world from which he wages war. Look at all the communication devices in the world today that receive transmissions through the air: television, radio, smartphones, social media, telecommunications, satellite technologies and a host of other media. Satan is a master deceiver, so the nations of the world have fallen under his influence, lies and deception.

What to do? It is time for the Church of Jesus Christ to stop believing everything they watch or read, and start using discernment, wisdom, biblical knowledge, prayer and vigilance. We should follow the well-known advice from Edgar Allan Poe: "Believe nothing you hear, and only one-half that you see."

Adam and Eve would have benefited from that advice in the Garden of Eden, being tempted by the serpent, who "was more crafty than any of the wild animals the LORD God had made" (Genesis 3:1).

The word *crafty* is *arum* in Hebrew, also defined as "cunning" or "shrewd," as in a poker game. Why was there a shrewd, crafty serpent talking to Eve? Where did it come from? While no one can state for sure the origins of deception, we do know we can trace it back to the fall of Lucifer before human history:

> "How you are fallen from heaven, O Lucifer, son of the morning! How you are cut down to the ground, you who weakened the nations! For you have said in your heart: 'I will ascend into heaven, I will exalt my throne above the stars of God; . . . I will ascend above the heights of the clouds, I will be like the Most High.' Yet you shall be brought down to Sheol, to the lowest depths of the Pit."
>
> Isaiah 14:12–15 NKJV

That Satan masquerades as an angel of light is not surprising since he was created to be a bright light in the heavens. (The Hebrew for *Lucifer* means "shining one, light-bearer.") It should also be no surprise that his goal is to deceive humankind into thinking there is no God and that life can be lived according to one's own intellect and emotional integrity. Some of the greatest thinkers of all times have espoused this deception.

About the Bible

Satan has repeated his challenge to Eve—"Did God really say?"—ever since the Fall. It is one of his greatest tactics to cause believers and unbelievers alike to question the nature of the Triune God (as we saw in the last chapter) and the authority of God's Word. Scholars and theologians state that there are contradictions and inconsistencies in Scripture, and that it cannot be the inerrant Word of God.

Here is Satan's tactic: If he can get pastors, leaders and laypeople to agree that the Bible has flaws, inconsistencies and contradictions, and that it is a judgmental book not to be believed, then he can end up unraveling our lives. This means *you* decide how you live, *you* decide what is sin and not sin. Believe and live however you want, since you can have no confidence in the Bible.

We can, however, trust the Bible for the following reasons:

- Fulfilled prophecies: Literally hundreds of prophecies written well before their fulfillment have been verified by history.
- Archaeological finds confirming the accuracy of the Bible.
- Manuscript evidence: The evidence of the Dead Sea Scrolls proves the reliability of the text.
- The Bible's proven track record of changing lives.

About Sin

Since, according to contemporary thinking, the Bible is out of date and out of sync with today's values, calling sin "sin" is judgmental—hate speech, even—and out of character with God, with love. Love, not the Bible, is the way to go. Even many who call themselves Christians believe that sin is whatever you make it out to be, according to your personal values.

These are lies from the pit of hell.

Paul Pickern, founder and CEO of All Pro Pastors International, a ministry that encourages and helps thousands of pastors, points out that many pastors have bought into the idea of "total tolerance" of sin:

> This has given way to them not preaching the whole Gospel and not preaching that there is an eternity with or without God. Hell is real, and an eternity without God is real, but the enemy has done a great job in getting us to the place that we cannot talk about eternity, other than everybody is going to heaven, or only about heaven. We know that's just a lie. It's not true.
>
> We've gotten into an attitude where we can't talk about certain things without offending someone. Sin is identified in the

Old Testament as well as the New Testament, and many people are going to die and go to hell. Many are active in a church because the church says, "Come as you are." They forget that when someone comes to Jesus, there is transformation; they become a new creature. This transformation has gotten lost in translation, with some forgetting that we walk away from the cross not bound to the sin that so easily besets us.[2]

Here is the truth: Sin is not you being out of alignment with your own values; it is you being out alignment with God's commands:

> Do you not know that the unrighteous will not inherit the kingdom of God? Do not be deceived. Neither fornicators, nor idolaters, nor adulterers, nor homosexuals, nor sodomites, nor thieves, nor covetous, nor drunkards, nor revilers, nor extortioners will inherit the kingdom of God. And such were some of you. But you were washed, but you were sanctified, but you were justified in the name of the Lord Jesus and by the Spirit of our God.
>
> 1 Corinthians 6:9–11 NKJV

About Salvation

Another deceptive lie: There are many paths to God. The Bible clearly states there is only one path to God and that is through Jesus Christ.

Here are just two key Scriptures:

> Jesus answered, "I am the way and the truth and the life. No one comes to the Father except through me."
>
> John 14:6

> Salvation is found in no one else, for there is no other name under heaven given to mankind by which we must be saved.
>
> Acts 4:12

If, however, we cannot trust the Bible as the infallible, inerrant Word of God, then we can come up with our own "salvation," our own philosophy on how we want to live. Who is there to prove us wrong?

Author and former pastor Lucas Miles, host of Faithwire's *The Lucas Miles Show* and co-host of *The Church Boys* podcast, where he has interviewed some of today's best-known media personalities, adds,

> When we fail to recognize that Scripture says, "There is no one righteous, not even one" (Romans 3:10), and we begin to think that we are somehow entitled to certain privileges on this earth, entitled to certain spiritual rewards, entitled to our salvation apart from Christ, apart from grace, apart from faith, then we've really entered into salvation by entitlement.
>
> This is what's behind a lot of the contrary ideas today, like certain theories about race. Basically it's a message of deservedness, contrary to the idea that I'm a sinner saved by grace, and that I rely on God for everything I have in this life. I think that is really creating an entitlement-based salvation mindset that is affecting believers on both the left and the right.[3]

How Do We Fight?

Lies, deception, chaos and doubt are prevalent. There are spiritually dark OPFOR at work in your community, workplace, city, state and nation. They are out to cause confusion, lies and misdirection in your life. How can you and your family battle these forces and come out victoriously?

By applying principles of biblical OPSEC.

Understanding the Battle

One principle is understanding the multidimensional nature of the battle.

Paul McGuire says, "We are fighting a spiritual battle, a political-economic battle and a psychological battle." He goes on,

> Most Christians don't understand that we have moved into a totally Orwellian and technological age where the average person's thoughts, beliefs and opinions can be manipulated through the internet, through social media, through computer systems, through algorithms, through sophisticated methodologies of mind control, through technologies of subtle hypnotic programming, and all kinds of technologies that you and I are exposed to on a daily basis that have been perfected over the last century.[4]

We must recognize Satan's final goal. According to Jesus in John 10:10, "The thief comes only to steal and kill and destroy; I have come that they may have life, and have it to the full."

This fascinating story from 1 Kings 22:19–23 gives insight into one of the ways the enemy achieves this goal. Only the godly prophet Micaiah, consulted by the kings of Israel and Judah, recognized the lie of the enemy, in contrast to the false prophets who were also consulted:

> Micaiah continued, "Therefore hear the word of the LORD: I saw the LORD sitting on his throne with all the multitudes of heaven standing around him on his right and on his left. And the LORD said, 'Who will entice Ahab into attacking Ramoth Gilead and going to his death there?' One suggested this, and another that. Finally, a spirit came forward, stood before the LORD and said, 'I will entice him.' 'By what means?' the LORD asked. 'I will go out and be a deceiving spirit in the mouths of all his prophets,' he said. 'You will succeed in enticing him,' said the LORD. 'Go and do it.'
>
> "So now the LORD has put a deceiving spirit in the mouths of all these prophets of yours. The LORD has decreed disaster for you."

That disaster happened. Because the kings of Israel and Judah listened to the lying spirit, the king of Israel was enticed and killed in battle.

Weaponized Wisdom

Another principle of biblical OPSEC is the way the U.S. Army fights opposing forces—by "a continuous process," which is an "inherent part of military culture and as such, must be fully integrated into the execution of all Army operations and supporting activities."[5]

What does this mean for us? That we must be always on guard, praying in the Spirit and asking God for discernment:

> This is my prayer: that your love may abound more and more in knowledge and depth of insight, so that you may be able to discern what is best and may be pure and blameless for the day of Christ, filled with the fruit of righteousness that comes through Jesus Christ—to the glory and praise of God.
>
> Philippians 1:9–11

What is discernment? We call it weaponized wisdom applied at the right time, place and target. At the heart of discernment is the love of the truth, as opposed to the love of a lie (see 2 Thessalonians 2:11–12).

A great definition of *discernment* comes from Ligonier Ministries:

> True discernment means not only distinguishing the right from the wrong; it means distinguishing the primary from the secondary, the essential from the indifferent, and the permanent from the transient. And, yes, it means distinguishing between the good and the better, and even between the better and the best.[6]

Discernment is God's gift to the Church to help us dispel confusion. Discernment can be a spiritual gift (see 1 Corinthians 12:10). It is also a skill that can be developed: "Solid food belongs to those who are of full age, that is, those who by reason of use have their senses exercised to discern both good and evil" (Hebrews 5:14 NKJV).

Biblical OPSEC might function for the believer like this in the following scenario:

You hear a sermon—maybe in person, maybe online—and you sense the Holy Spirit telling you that something is not quite right. You immediately go into action, ask the Lord for discernment and dig into the Word of God. And you find that the pastor was not preaching biblical truth.

Jerry Moses, assistant to the president at Movieguide, former assistant to the president at Christian Broadcasting Network, former pastor of several large churches in California and Oregon and advisor to Battle Ready Ministries, deplores that some churches are no longer preaching the "whole counsel of God" (Acts 20:27 NKJV) and the Bible as the inerrant Word of God.

> What is under attack today, which is going to bring us to the end times, is the Bible being thrown out by people saying that it is not the Word of God. The Bible, they say, has no authority; it's just literature. They are taking away the authority of God speaking and the presence of the Holy Spirit, who wrote the Bible. Without that, there is no conviction of sin and no salvation.
>
> People in history have been burned at the stake for nothing more than saying the Bible is the Word of God. It has to be primary in the Church.[7]

International evangelist and bestselling author Mario Murillo believes that some churches have become "compromised clubs," and that to stop losing ground to the enemy, "we must stop playing church." He appeals to one of the lessons from the life of German pastor and theologian Dietrich Bonhoeffer, hanged by the Nazis in 1945:

> Sadly, one of the things that messed [the Church] up is what Bonhoeffer said: "If you want to understand how Hitler came to power . . . it was cheap grace." . . . Now the cheap grace message set up the American Christian on a very specific level. It wasn't so much that they believed they could enjoy forgiveness without repentance, which is utterly wrong. It was . . . the idea that from this point on, nothing that I find uncomfortable has to be from God because of His grace. So the issue of consequence [for sin] went out the window. And so [pastors] saw that if preaching sin to America is uncomfortable, I won't do it, because of grace.[8]

At a time when the forces of darkness are coming after our freedom and force-feeding our children the Antichrist agenda, Murillo says God is offering protection for those waking up to their purpose and destiny in the last days before Christ's return. As Jesus told the Laodicean church, which was "wretched, pitiful, poor, blind and naked" (Revelation 3:17), "Here I am! I stand at the door and knock. If anyone hears my voice and opens the door, I will come in and eat with that person, and they with me" (verse 20).

Murillo sums it up:

> This is the paradox of the hour. God is affording us an intimacy with Him that has not been available to prior generations. God is saying, "Just as they are delving into dramatic evil and wickedness, you can enjoy intimacy and righteousness with God, and a peace that passes understanding." But not if we don't open the door. We have to open the door, and He will come in. And all of these tremendous blessings of the last days will be unfolded.[9]

TACTICS, TECHNIQUES
AND PROCEDURES

Use the following strategies to combat deception and exercise discernment.

1. **Test the spirits.** "Do not believe every spirit, but test the spirits to see whether they are from God, because many false prophets have gone out into the world" (1 John 4:1). Ask God continually if what you are hearing and seeing is of Him or of the lies of the world. It might be the messages you listen to in person or online. Do your own research and find out the truth. Do they line up with the Bible? Are they consistent with the whole counsel of God?

2. **Test yourself.** Just as the Army tests its soldiers and their equipment regularly, "Examine yourselves to see whether you are in the faith. . . . Do you not realize that Christ Jesus is in you—unless, of course, you fail the test?" (2 Corinthians 13:5). Do you believe that Jesus is fully God and fully Man, the Lord of lords and King of kings? Are you willing to follow Him wherever He leads, even though opposing forces try to stop you?

3. **Test your desire to seek Him.** "You will seek me and find me when you seek me with all your heart" (Jeremiah 29:13). Do this by applying the Word of God every day—at your job, in your home, with your family and with your friends. To discern God's voice, you must be seeking Him. Be intentional and fervent about seeking Him.

5

Psychological Operations

Truth lives on in the midst of deception.
FRIEDRICH VON SCHILLER,
"Ode to Joy"

FALL 2005
BAGHDAD, IRAQ

"No more B-52s, no more B-52s."

We kept hearing this phrase over and over from Iraqis running up to us, shouting, hands waving, whether in Baghdad or in other parts of the country.

Years before, during Operation Desert Storm, the U.S. used the mighty Air Force bomber B-52H Stratofortress, which had dropped tons of munitions on the Republican Guard over wide areas of Iraq. Those unfortunate Iraqis must at one time have been in the Republican Guard and probably never really knew what a B-52H Stratofortress was, but the very name put fear in them even years later.

The truth is, those guys never even saw a B-52H Stratofortress since they fly so high (up to fifty thousand feet), but they

69

wanted no more of them. The psychological damage alone did enough to keep them afraid years after the event.

In the same way, we need to be aware in these last days of what the Army calls psychological operations (PSYOP). Here is the definition in the U.S. Army *Field Manual*:

> PSYOP are planned operations that convey selected information and indicators to foreign target audiences (TAs) to influence their emotions, motives, objective reasoning, and ultimately, the behavior of foreign governments, organizations, groups, and individuals. The purpose of all PSYOP is to create in neutral, friendly, or hostile foreign groups the emotions, attitudes, or desired behavior that support the achievement of U.S. national objectives and the military mission.[1]

To win wars, the military must go out into the communities and influence the local populace to support it, or else convince enemy combatants that it is in their best interests not to fight. Sometimes military commanders will offer jobs, education or other incentives to persuade a populace.

The *Field Manual* adds that "tactical PSYOP forces provide supported commanders a nonlethal fires capability to change the behavior of a local populace or adversary force in any environment."[2] "Nonlethal fires capability" means using other means besides killing to get the enemy to stop fighting and offer support.

The forces of darkness use PSYOP tactics increasingly effectively against the Church.

Various PSYOP Attacks

Many of today's pressing social ills, upheaval and seemingly intractable political problems are rooted in the Church's failure to take a stand for the Word of God and the Person and work of Jesus Christ, and in the PSYOP attacks of the enemy.

Fear

Many pastors are afraid of criticism, in contrast to what Jesus stated in Matthew 5:11–12:

"Blessed are you when people insult you, persecute you and falsely say all kinds of evil against you because of me. Rejoice and be glad, because great is your reward in heaven, for in the same way they persecuted the prophets who were before you."

Pastors can fear the culture, the government, other religions, even their own congregations. Many believe that if they start preaching unpopular subjects like holiness, hell, heaven, the Second Coming, sin and righteousness, they will be shunned by their people and the society around them. This subtle attack is none other than our archenemy employing PSYOP against the Church.

Pastors may fear what the cancel culture's PSYOP may do to their reputations or their churches. Or they are nervous about losing their tax-exempt status or about governmental regulations that would hinder their ministry.

Progressive Ideologies

Author, former pastor and critical-theory expert Lucas Miles says many Christians today have embraced progressive ideologies, even Marxist theory:

I think many, especially in the evangelical world, are being enchanted by this and drawn into their belief system. It is pervasive today in the Church. Many of these individuals are not familiar with Marx. They haven't read [philosopher Georg] Hegel. They're not militant about their beliefs, but they've adopted a more progressive view of faith. As individuals are drawn away from the Bible as their source of truth, it creates opportunity for them to start adopting extrabiblical ideas that are antithetical to

Scripture, like pro-choice doctrines, subscribing to an LGBTQ agenda, supporting same-sex marriage, Marxist theory and much more.[3]

Lack of Discernment

We talked in the last chapter about the need for discernment—for example, when you hear something taught and sense the Holy Spirit saying that something is not quite right. You ask the Lord for discernment and dig into the Word of God—and find that the pastor is not preaching biblical truth.

Is your church biblically sound? Does it preach feel-good theology or challenge you to become a close follower of Christ? Does the pastor preach the entire Word of God, even the difficult subjects of hell, sin, obedience, persecution, holiness and Bible prophecy? What are the doctrines or beliefs of the leadership? Do they conform to cultural expectations and political correctness, or do they hold to the timeless, historic, tested core doctrines of the Church that include salvation by faith and grace, the infallible Word of God, Jesus as both God and Man, the power of the Holy Spirit and His enabling gifts, the doctrine of the Trinity and much more?

Coco Perez, lead pastor of Horizon Church in West Sacramento, California, and a board advisor to Battle Ready Ministries, says,

> Some pastors study the Bible; others prepare sermons. In today's church environment, the sermon pastor prepares to please, to comfort people and to make them feel good. I get it; it's okay sometimes. But it's not healthy for the long run.
>
> The pastor who studies the Bible gets the whole picture and provides fresh revelation of who God is. Hebrews 11:6 says, "Without faith it is impossible to please God, because anyone who comes to him must believe that he exists and that he rewards those who earnestly seek him."[4]

Are there small "life groups" through which you can connect spiritually with others? Are there those connected to this church who can provide sound biblical guidance and advice? Great discernment is needed in these end times.

The Bifurcation PSYOP

One of the great psychological operations against the Church today is called bifurcation. Simply put, this is the division between the secular and the sacred. Some Christians think it is okay to live one way in church and another way during the week. They do not let their faith inform their decisions during the week.

Author and social critic Os Guinness comments,

> Many Christians have a faith too privatized. Privately engaging, publicly irrelevant. It's not integrated. They're not making Jesus Lord of the whole of life. They've got to get over that. We have got to engage the whole of life in our callings.[5]

One example of bifurcation is found in the book of Acts, soon after the great outpouring of the Holy Spirit. Ananias and Sapphira wanted to impress the disciples by donating the proceeds from the sale of a piece of property. But they pretended to give the entire amount while keeping some of the money for themselves.

> Peter said, "Ananias, how is it that Satan has so filled your heart that you have lied to the Holy Spirit and have kept for yourself some of the money you received for the land? Didn't it belong to you before it was sold? And after it was sold, wasn't the money at your disposal? What made you think of doing such a thing? You have not lied just to human beings but to God." When Ananias heard this, he fell down and died. And great fear seized all who heard what had happened.
>
> Acts 5:3–5

His wife subsequently told the same lie to Peter about three hours later, and also fell down dead.

Ananias and Sapphira did not allow their faith to inform their decision, instead lying to the apostles. Bad choice.

In my own profession as a senior-level chaplain, I got to minister to chaplains and their assistants, almost on a weekly basis, who had also made bad choices and veered off the moral path into financial and sexual ruin.

There are no perfect people. But pastors are the most targeted by the enemy. Many have slid into moral failure. Others have fallen from biblical authority and are teaching heresy and deception from the pulpit. In the end times, this will continue to happen at an alarming rate.

We have come to a crossroads. If we sit and do nothing, then the observation inspired by English philosopher John Stuart Mill will come true: "The only thing necessary for the triumph of evil is for good men to do nothing." We must—like the black-robed preachers of the American Revolution who inspired and fought alongside their congregations in the battle against British tyranny—take a firm stand against the rise of dark powers. Not only must we become spiritually battle ready, but pastors must lead the way and train their congregations.

The Bible says that Jesus is to be Lord over all our lives, in everything we do and in everything we become.

The False Religion PSYOP

Another psychological tool of the enemy that will play a key role in the last days is deception in the form of false religions around the world.

Evangelical pollster George Barna finds Christianity declining while atheism continues to increase. By 2018 Christianity in the United States had dropped significantly, from 81 percent in 2003 to 72 percent, while the percentage of atheists, agnostics and those of no religion ("nones") nearly doubled from 11 percent in 2003 to 21 percent in 2018.[6]

The fastest-growing religion in the U.S. is Wicca,[7] modern paganism practicing witchcraft and nature worship.

The fastest-growing religion in the world is Islam.[8] It is growing because it is devout, and because many are looking for a religion that tells them how to live, and because many Muslims have large families.

Early every morning at Khobar Towers in Dhahran, Saudi Arabia, I heard the call to prayer from a nearby mosque, every day without fail, five times a day. Islam is a very public and outward religion.

There was something different in that land—different smells, different views and a darkness I still cannot shake. Many of the Muslims I knew were good people; they were friendly and just wanted to live quiet and peaceable lives. At the same time, there are radical fundamentalists who see the West, especially America, as decadent, and want to kill everyone who does not agree with their religion and way of life.

Many ask Troy and me, "How can you be sure the Christian 'religion' is the right one, since there are many religions in the world that claim they are the correct religion?" Our answer is simple: How many of the leaders of those religions have been resurrected from the dead and are no longer in the grave?

Christianity is not another religion; it is a relationship with the living Christ, who is soon to return to this earth.

Before that time, the armed forces of the Antichrist

> will rise up to desecrate the temple fortress and will abolish the daily sacrifice. Then they will set up the abomination that causes desolation. With flattery he will corrupt those who have violated the covenant, but the people who know their God will firmly resist him.
>
> Daniel 11:31–32

We have already seen from Revelation 13 that the Antichrist can "cause all who refused to worship the image to be killed" (verse 15).

These chapters of the Bible reveal one undeniable fact: The Antichrist will, during the Great Tribulation, walk into the rebuilt Temple in Jerusalem, end the daily sacrifices and proclaim himself to be God. He will cause the world to worship him, and if you decide that is not for you, you will be put to death.

Bottom line: Whether you believe the Antichrist will come out of Europe or the Middle East, whether he will dominate the whole world or just the greater part of the Middle East, the fact remains that he will demand to be worshiped as God, placing great fear and distress on the whole world. False religious beliefs will thus play a great role in deceiving the whole earth.

Standing against PSYOP

The question arises: How to counter these psychological operations?

It is essential to determine whether a church or ministry is in alignment with God's Word. Despite variations in theology and practice, one way to do this is using as a plumbline the time-honored and traditional Apostles' Creed. This creed was developed in the fourth or fifth century and lays out simple but mainstream Christian doctrine:

> I believe in God, the Father almighty,
> creator of heaven and earth.
>
> I believe in Jesus Christ, his only Son, our Lord,
> who was conceived by the Holy Spirit,
> born of the Virgin Mary,
> suffered under Pontius Pilate,
> was crucified, died, and was buried;
> he descended to the dead.

On the third day he rose again;
he ascended into heaven,
he is seated at the right hand of the Father,
and he will come to judge the living and the dead.

I believe in the Holy Spirit,
the holy catholic Church,
the communion of saints,
the forgiveness of sins,
the resurrection of the body,
and the life everlasting.
Amen.[9]

The phrase *holy catholic Church* refers not to the Roman Catholic Church but to the Body of Christ in every time and place. This creed helps center us on the essential doctrines of the Church. It is important not only to believe these doctrines, but to practice them in everyday life. It keeps our focus on God, not man, and it guards us against false doctrine and sliding into deception.

TACTICS, TECHNIQUES AND PROCEDURES

A Joint Chiefs of Staff publication lays out principles of military deception that provide guidance for PSYOP, which we can use as followers of Christ.[10] Here are three of those principles:

1. **Focus.** "Where there is no counsel, the people fall; but in the multitude of counselors there is safety" (Proverbs 11:14 NKJV). The military focuses on the decision-makers who can change the outcome of the battle. Our focus as leaders must be making biblically sound decisions for the

group God has placed under us. Make it a practice every day to read a proverb or a chapter from Proverbs and implement it in your home.

2. **Objective.** A key military goal is to cause the adversary not just to believe certain things, but to take (or not take) specific actions. Satan will try to cause you to believe falsehoods and distract you from your objective. What is your objective? It is to follow Christ every moment of every day. "Come, follow me," Jesus said (Matthew 4:19). A good way to start every day is allowing the Bible to speak to you and then implementing it in your life.

3. **Security.** The military does all it can to protect its intent, position and power so the enemy cannot know what it is about to do. In the same way, we must guard our hearts against the onslaught of the enemy, of the culture and of everything surrounding our Christian faith. "The Spirit God gave us does not make us timid, but gives us power, love and self-discipline" (2 Timothy 1:7). Praying in the Spirit is a powerful tool that we must utilize in the end times. We protect ourselves by using the shield of faith described in Ephesians 6:16. Faith is our unswerving, unflinching and firm belief in God's Word. If God said it, we must hold fast to His promises.

6

Center of Operations

The Scripture says that a Great Dictator is coming and he will
be boosted to power, and strengthened in his grasp upon the
world with the assistance of the ancient religion called Mystery,
Babylon. This is the very religion which started in the Genesis
account and made possible the first world dictator.

HAL LINDSEY, *The Late Great Planet Earth*

OCTOBER 2005
TALLIL AIR BASE (NOW IMAM ALI AIR BASE)
SOUTHERN IRAQ

My chaplains and assistants and I are gathered on top of the
Great Ziggurat of Ur for training. The area is not totally secure;
enemy combatants have been seen in the area, so we have security set up. Later we find out the area is closed off for security
reasons. Our training is centered on the religious and cultural
history of Iraq so we can give our commanders better insights
and intelligence on the area.

This ancient ziggurat with a temple on top is a massive, ter-
raced structure that can be seen by astronauts in outer space

and is more than four thousand years old. And today we have a rare treat: One of our chaplain assistants is a Ph.D. candidate writing his dissertation on this temple.

As I stand atop this ziggurat, I marvel that Ur is the city Abraham was from, which God called him to leave in order to "go . . . to the land I will show you" (Genesis 12:1). And I reflect on the importance of this ziggurat to the civilization surrounding it and its role in spiritual deception throughout the millennia.

Dr. Senta German, formerly of the Ashmolean Museum of Art and Archaeology at Oxford, described this structure as the center of life for Ur and the surrounding area:

> The Ziggurat at Ur and the temple on its top were built around 2100 B.C.E. by the king Ur-Nammu of the Third Dynasty of Ur for the moon goddess Nanna, the divine patron of the city state. The structure would have been the highest point in the city by far and, like the spire of a medieval cathedral, would have been visible for miles around, a focal point for travelers and the pious alike. As the Ziggurat supported the temple of the patron god of the city of Ur, it is likely that it was the place where the citizens of Ur would bring agricultural surplus and where they would go to receive their regular food allotments. In antiquity, to visit the ziggurat at Ur was to seek both spiritual and physical nourishment.[1]

This ziggurat, then, was the center of life for the people of Ur. It was also the headquarters for religious deception in that land many years ago. It was the focus of goddess worship there and played a significant role in leading people astray.

The Significance of Babel

Every military organization has a system and structure reflecting its need for hierarchy, leadership, safety and centrality. The headquarters of the U.S. military is the Pentagon, found near the capital of the United States, Washington, D.C.

The Pentagon (to which I was assigned for four years) is a five-sided building built during World War II. It is still the world's largest office building with 17.5 miles of corridors and 3.7 million square feet of office space. It is the headquarters of the U.S. Department of Defense, and where most strategic military decisions are made.

The importance of a headquarters to any military organization cannot be overstated. Each echelon or level in the U.S. Army, for instance, starting with a battalion, has a command-and-control center to facilitate order, leadership and control of the battle or war. The doctrines by which an Army headquarters operates is clearly stated in the field manuals produced by the Army's Training and Doctrine Command. Having the correct doctrine is imperative for winning the war!

Just as the Pentagon is the headquarters for the U.S. military, and the Great Ziggurat of Ur was the center of operations for the people of Ur, another ziggurat on the plain in Shinar in ancient Babel (also in today's Iraq) had deep spiritual significance.

The Tower of Babel was a religious shrine intended to reach the heavens and usurp God's dominion. God disrupted the construction of the Tower of Babel by confusing the languages of the workers so they could no longer understand one another. The city and tower were not completed, and the people eventually dispersed. Let's read the story in Genesis 11:1–9:

> Now the whole world had one language and a common speech. As people moved eastward, they found a plain in Shinar and settled there.
>
> They said to each other, "Come, let's make bricks and bake them thoroughly." They used brick instead of stone, and tar for mortar. Then they said, "Come, let us build ourselves a city, with a tower that reaches to the heavens, so that we may make

a name for ourselves; otherwise we will be scattered over the face of the whole earth."

But the LORD came down to see the city and the tower the people were building. The LORD said, "If as one people speaking the same language they have begun to do this, then nothing they plan to do will be impossible for them. Come, let us go down and confuse their language so they will not understand each other."

So the LORD scattered them from there over all the earth, and they stopped building the city. That is why it was called Babel—because there the LORD confused the language of the whole world. From there the LORD scattered them over the face of the whole earth.

The Tower of Babel is closely linked to one of the greatest deceptions in Scripture. That ziggurat, built in rebellion against God, was to be a center of false worship and the economic and political capital of the ancient world—a world that, not long after the global destruction of Noah's flood, was already leaving God out of the picture. Because God in His wisdom knew they would destroy themselves and that it was not time for the world to end yet, He scattered them across the globe.

Today we are seeing the rise of what the apostle John in the book of Revelation called "Mystery Babylon," a global economic, political and religious system that will be built around the Antichrist, false religion, humanism, the occult and life without God—paralleling what happened at the Tower of Babel. Here is what John saw:

Then one of the seven angels who had the seven bowls came and talked with me, saying to me, "Come, I will show you the judgment of the great harlot who sits on many waters, with whom the kings of the earth committed fornication, and the inhabitants of the earth were made drunk with the wine of her fornication."

So he carried me away in the Spirit into the wilderness. And I saw a woman sitting on a scarlet beast which was full of names of blasphemy, having seven heads and ten horns. The woman was arrayed in purple and scarlet, and adorned with gold and precious stones and pearls, having in her hand a golden cup full of abominations and the filthiness of her fornication. And on her forehead a name was written:

Mystery, Babylon the great, the mother of harlots and of the abominations of the earth.

I saw the woman, drunk with the blood of the saints and with the blood of the martyrs of Jesus. And when I saw her, I marveled with great amazement. . . .

Then he said to me, "The waters which you saw, where the harlot sits, are peoples, multitudes, nations, and tongues. And the ten horns which you saw on the beast, these will hate the harlot, make her desolate and naked, eat her flesh and burn her with fire. For God has put it into their hearts to fulfill His purpose, to be of one mind, and to give their kingdom to the beast, until the words of God are fulfilled. And the woman whom you saw is that great city which reigns over the kings of the earth."

Revelation 17:1–6, 15–18 NKJV

The Tower of Babel story is the genesis of humanity's attempts throughout history—including the Babylonian Empire, the Medo-Persian Empire, the Greek Empire and the Roman Empire—to unite the world in rebellion against God. More than one hundred passages of Scripture indicate that the Antichrist, under the direction of Satan, will rule a one-world governmental, economic and religious system in the end times.[2]

Retired U.S. Army Chaplain (Col.) Peter Brzezinski sees the spirit behind the Tower of Babel as one of the greatest deceptions in the world. It is the lie that says, "If we can just get together and put out enough effort, humanly speaking, leaving

God out of the picture, we can accomplish anything." Brzezinski goes on to explain that

> God looked down and said, "If man can get together and decide to do this, nothing will be impossible to them. I need to go down and confuse them." It's the same lie of 2 Thessalonians 2:11: "God sends them a powerful delusion so that they will believe the lie." So I see the spirit of the Tower of Babel—all this knowledge being raised up against the knowledge of God—as one of the greatest deceptions in the world today. We think we don't need God. In fact, God is in the way; we can do it ourselves.[3]

The Three Temples

Another temple of religious significance—this one in Jerusalem, inspired by love for God—served as the religious headquarters in the life of the Jews. It is the centerpiece of Bible prophecy in the end times.

The splendid first Temple, ordained by God Himself, was designed by King David and built in Jerusalem by King Solomon around 957 BC. It was destroyed by King Nebuchadnezzar and the Babylonians around 587 BC after standing more than five hundred years.[4]

The second Temple was built in the same location by Zerubbabel, governor of Jerusalem, in 515 BC. Herod the Great, before and during the time of Jesus, undertook a massive transformation and expansion of the Temple so that it rivaled any of the architecture of Rome at that time. It was destroyed in AD 70 by the Roman general Titus and the Tenth Roman Legion.[5]

The third Temple will be rebuilt in the end times, and the Antichrist will enter the Temple in the middle of the Great Tribulation and proclaim himself to be God. As the angel told Daniel,

"The end will come like a flood: War will continue until the end, and desolations have been decreed. He will confirm a covenant with many for one 'seven.' In the middle of the 'seven' he will put an end to sacrifice and offering. And at the temple he will set up an abomination that causes desolation, until the end that is decreed is poured out on him."

Daniel 9:26–27

Traditionally (and Troy and I agree) the "covenant" referred to is interpreted as an alliance that the Antichrist will make with Israel for seven years. Then he will break that covenant and enter the third Temple, stop the ritual sacrifices and set up an image for the world to worship as he proclaims himself to be God.

This is when, according to Revelation 13:11–17, the Antichrist (or the Beast) forces all people to receive a mark in order to buy and sell.

Still far in the future? Maybe not. Donna Howell and Allie Henson write in *Dark Covenant* about the announcement made in 2020 by the World Economic Forum of an initiative called "the great reset."[6] With the push toward a cashless society, and what some are calling the emergence of a "global super-religion combining key aspects of all faiths into one,"[7] these authors think we may be witnessing the initial stages of the coming global Antichrist system. They explain,

If it plays out the way most Bible prophecy theologians suggest it will, Antichrist will live up to his title in every literal way. As the "anti" form of our Savior, Christ, the Man of Sin will parallel Jesus' death, resurrection, and miracles, looking in every way to be the Messiah figure for all world religions and cultures across the globe: Jews will believe he is the promised Messiah they've waited for; misled Christians will believe it is the Second Coming of Christ; people belonging to other world religions will interpret him to be the fulfillment of other prophetic, redeeming, or delivering god-figures; and atheists will suddenly come to believe that there is a God—and that Antichrist fills the role.[8]

Peter Brzezinski also sees the Antichrist as

the person to come who is going to be a "savior" that is not Christ, a person who will do mighty and great things, but the power behind that person is evil.

One interpretation of the end times is that there has to be a Temple to be built for people to be drawn to, but it will not be positive; it will be false. One of the signs is that they will want to reinstate the old sacrificial system, ignoring the ultimate sacrifice of Christ.[9]

The Third Temple

The Temple in Jerusalem always has been a very important edifice—we might say "the center of operations"—for the Jewish faithful. Not only will it be rebuilt in the end times, but the Temple will be the very centerpiece of the prophetic calendar.

Troy and I think a deception is being played out right now, in that most Jews and the chief rabbis believe that the third Temple will be built on what is currently the Dome of the Rock, located on the Temple Mount in the Old City of Jerusalem. Most Jews, especially the ultra-Orthodox, worship and pray at the Western Wall, or the Wailing Wall—what is believed to be the remnants of the outer wall of the second Temple. No rabbi will even discuss the possibility of another location. They believe the Dome of the Rock was built over the Holy of Holies of the second Temple.

Rabbi Jonathan Bernis, president and CEO of Jewish Voice Ministries International and host of the globally syndicated television show *Jewish Voice with Jonathan Bernis*, clarifies the delicacy of rebuilding in that location:

> No one in the Islamic world would ever, in the natural, agree to rebuilding the Temple alongside the Dome of the Rock, or for the Dome to come down—not just radicals, but any practicing Muslim, since that's the second-holiest site for them. So anyone who could negotiate that and make it happen would, I think, have the clearest credentials of being the Antichrist.[10]

There is mounting evidence, however, that the actual location of the first and second Temples was in the City of David, by the Gihon Spring and Pool of Siloam, south of the Temple Mount. One large body of evidence is found in a book called *The Temples that Jerusalem Forgot* by Dr. Ernest L. Martin. He and a number of other scholars and archaeologists have assembled a formidable collection of support and primary documents that attest to this.

There is another school of thought that the third Temple could possibly be built north of the Dome of the Rock directly over the Dome of the Spirits and in line with the Golden Gate, facing east.[11]

Wherever the third Temple is built, we know it will signify the rise of the Antichrist, possibly meaning that it will *not* be on the Dome of the Rock—apart from the diplomatic success of the Antichrist, which Rabbi Bernis points out—because of the extreme likelihood of a major war with Islam, possibly World War III.

Having said that, however, we cannot underestimate what God will do in the future. That is the reason Jesus told us to watch and pray.

Although Jesus considered the Temple "my Father's house" (John 2:16), He predicted its destruction in Matthew 24:2. That prophecy was fulfilled just forty years later, in AD 70. For more than two thousand years, devout Jews have waited for the rebuilding of their Temple.

Troy and I think the announcement for building the third Temple will set in motion a whole series of events leading to the beginning of the end, the ultimate prophetic countdown and the return of Jesus Christ to set up His Kingdom.

Replacement Theology

Some scholars and Christian leaders believe that the Church is the new Israel. This view is called supersessionism, replacement theology or fulfillment theology. The gist of this thought is as follows:

> Supersessionism is the view that the NT church is the new and/or true Israel that has forever superseded the nation Israel as the people of God. It may take the form of "punitive supersessionism," i.e., God is punishing Israel for her rejection of Christ. Or it may be in the form of "economic supersessionism," i.e., it was God's plan for Israel's role as the people of God to expire with the coming of Christ and be replaced by the church.[12]

Arguments over whether the Church is the "replacement" for Israel have been ongoing for two thousand years. The danger of the doctrine of supersessionism is that it has spurred anti-Semitism throughout Church history, and the deception is that it does not align with Scripture. Here is part of the covenant God made with Abraham:

> "To your descendants I give this land, from the Wadi of Egypt to the great river, the Euphrates—the land of the Kenites, Kenizzites, Kadmonites, Hittites, Perizzites, Rephaites, Amorites, Canaanites, Girgashites and Jebusites."

Genesis 15:18–21

The covenant is reinforced in Jeremiah 31:35–36:

> This is what the LORD says, he who appoints the sun to shine by day, who decrees the moon and stars to shine by night, who stirs up the sea so that its waves roar—the LORD Almighty is his name: "Only if these decrees vanish from my sight," declares the LORD, "will Israel ever cease being a nation before me."

God's unconditional (absolute) oath to Abraham has not changed, because His oath did not depend on what Israel did or did not do; it depended completely on God and what He would do with Israel.

Jesus' Glorious Return

Where is Jesus coming back? Not to North America, Europe or Asia. Zechariah 14:4–5 describes His destination and this glorious event:

> On that day his feet will stand on the Mount of Olives, east of Jerusalem, and the Mount of Olives will be split in two from east to west, forming a great valley, with half of the mountain moving north and half moving south. . . . Then the LORD my God will come, and all the holy ones with him.

Yes, Jesus will set foot on the Mount of Olives and establish His new headquarters in Jerusalem, where He will rule during the Millennium and where all the nations of the earth will gather to worship Him.

> At that time they will call Jerusalem The Throne of the LORD, and all nations will gather in Jerusalem to honor the name of the LORD. No longer will they follow the stubbornness of their evil hearts.
>
> Jeremiah 3:17

Your Center of Operations

We have seen that every military organization has a headquarters. So it is with us. All followers of Jesus need a headquarters, a center of operations, to unite us in the faith and in our lives. The foundations Satan is fighting against—the Church and the family—are the foundations we need more than ever before.

Think about the headquarters in your life, especially your family and your church, as you read this passage from Ephesians:

> You are no longer foreigners and strangers, but fellow citizens with God's people and also members of his household, built on the foundation of the apostles and prophets, with Christ Jesus himself as the chief cornerstone. In him the whole building is joined together and rises to become a holy temple in the Lord. And in him you too are being built together to become a dwelling in which God lives by his Spirit.
>
> Ephesians 2:19–22

You are part of Jesus' holy temple, and He is the chief cornerstone holding your life, your family and your church together for His glory.

Your operational headquarters must be your home, where you read the Bible, pray, worship the Lord, conduct Bible studies, minister the Gospel to your family, extend hospitality and enjoy fellowship with those you love. The importance of your home cannot be underestimated.

Fight, then, to maintain this headquarters in your life. Following are some strategies to do this.

TACTICS, TECHNIQUES
AND PROCEDURES

1. **Read about the Jewish Temple** in the Scriptures, especially the third Temple about to be built. Here are some to start with: Daniel 9:24–27; Daniel 11:31; Matthew 24:15; and 2 Thessalonians 2:1–12.

2. **Think about your personal headquarters,** especially your family and church. How important are they to you? If they are less important than they should be, what needs to happen to make them a priority? Read and study Ephesians 2:19–22.

3. **Study God's covenant with Abraham.** How does the covenant God made with Abraham (see Genesis 15) apply to your life today, given that it centers around Israel and the Jews?

4. **Watch the news and other sources** for the possible building of the third Temple in Jerusalem. This will strengthen your faith, help you realize the closeness of the coming of the Lord and enable you to "stand up and lift up your heads, because your redemption is drawing near" (Luke 21:28).

PART 2

DECEPTION IN THE WORLD SYSTEM

7

Night-Vision Goggles

Those who do not learn history are doomed to repeat it.

GEORGE SANTAYANA, philosopher,
essayist and poet

WINTER 2006
CAMP BALAD, SOUTHERN IRAQ
NIGHT

I am headed back to my hooch after a long, grueling day of training and counseling soldiers. As I walk between convoy vehicles preparing to go out on patrol, a soldier on top of the first vehicle sees me and apparently notices that I have a cross on my Kevlar vest.

He shouts down to me, "Chaplain, would you say a prayer for us before we head out on night convoy operation?"

"Of course I will," I say. And I stop and pray for their safety and quick return.

As I continue on my way, I look up at the stars blanketing the night sky. Breathtaking! I have plenty of time to think.

The desert night covers the landscape with darkness so thick you cannot see. Really, I ponder, it is like the darkness that has covered recorded human history for the past five thousand–plus years.

But one invention in the darkness has changed the equation of nighttime warfare. The military that has night-vision goggles (NVGs) owns the night. With that kind of hardware, you can see the enemy when the enemy is unable to see you, and the side that owns the darkness wins the fight.

Darkness and Deception

Until recent years, darkness covered potential enemies hiding in obscurity. But because we now can see at night, the darkness becomes known and is no longer a threat.

It is the same in the spiritual order. The Word of God shines light in the darkness, exposing it for what it really is. The psalmist wrote, "Your word is a lamp for my feet, a light on my path" (Psalm 119:105).

At Fort Ord on Monterey Bay in California, I was assigned to an infantry unit for two weeks of light fighter training with the 7th Infantry Division. At one point with NVGs on, I stood in the middle of the road with two columns of infantry soldiers marching toward me. They passed me on each side without knowing I was there! They did not have NVGs with them for that event. I did.

Darkness and deception go hand in hand. If only we had spiritual NVGs to see the deception all around us! But we have better than night-vision goggles; we have the Holy Spirit, who gives us discernment, and we have the Word of God, inspired by the Holy Spirit, which gives us light and direction in the dark.

Dr. Robert Jeffress, senior pastor of First Baptist Church in Dallas, says,

Nothing cuts through the fog of deception quicker than the Word of God. Ephesians 6:10–18, which talks about the armor that God has provided for every Christian, also talks about taking up the sword of the Spirit. Hebrews 4:12 says the Word of God is alive and active and sharper than any double-edged sword. Unfortunately, too many Christians are too unfamiliar with God's Word. They have no idea of its power or even of its content. I think that's why you find so many Christians falling for the deception of the evil one.[1]

Darkness and deception, from the beginning of human history, have played a key part in the life of humankind. It is interesting to note that Adam and Eve were created perfect in every way, yet they still fell to the lies of the serpent in the Garden of Eden:

"You will not certainly die," the serpent said to the woman. "For God knows that when you eat from it your eyes will be opened, and you will be like God, knowing good and evil."

Genesis 3:4–5

This lie of the evil one—that Adam and Eve would "not certainly die"—led to universal sin and death, and the need for God to send His Son to die in our place to bring us back into relationship with Him.

Other kinds of deception have also led to death. Revisionist history is a dangerous form of deception since if we do not learn from history, we are doomed to repeat it. Here is an example.

Over the decades some have called the Holocaust in World War II a myth and claimed that not that many Jews died in Nazi extermination camps—or even that there were no such camps at all. The fact is, some six million Jews were murdered systematically in those camps. But some people have believed the lie of Holocaust denial, and today anti-Semitism is on the rise, especially in Europe and the Middle East.

Revisionists want to do away with history so they can have their way and bring about their own insidious plans.

Godly government is a gift. But much of our current culture has forgotten history—that Communism, socialism, fascism or any other kind of total government control has never worked and never will. Why? Because of the inclination of those in charge to hoard all the money and power. And not only those in charge. All we need to do is look at the Bible to find the truth about all human beings: "The heart is deceitful above all things and beyond cure. Who can understand it?" (Jeremiah 17:9).

Let's put on our spiritual NVGs, then, and expose three of the deceptions out there.

Critical Race Theory (CRT)

Critical race theory is defined by Britannica as an

intellectual and social movement . . . based on the premise that race is not a natural, biologically grounded feature of physically distinct subgroups of human beings but a socially constructed (culturally invented) category that is used to oppress and exploit people of colour.[2]

One of the originators of CRT, Derrick A. Bell, wrote, "As I see it, critical race theory recognizes that revolutionizing a culture begins with the radical assessment of it."[3] Most CRT advocates have not only assessed culture radically but want to change it by divisiveness, anarchy and revolution—the same practices seen throughout the history of socialism and Communism.

The Heritage Foundation, a conservative think tank, points out that CRT has its roots in the Institute for Social Research in Germany, the Marxist school that is also the origin of cancel culture and wokeism (as we discussed in chapter 2). Jonathan Butcher explains that critical race theory

> approaches everything through the prism of race. All aspects of American life are seen in terms of racial power dynamics, and because critical race theory scholars have been so persistent, critical race theory is now impacting all aspects of American life. The protests of 2020, the riots, the inclusion of racial dynamics in everything from schools to sports to corporate boards, are all the result of critical race theory.[4]

Butcher goes on to write with Mike Gonzales that "CRT is purposely political and dispenses with the idea of rights because it blames all inequalities of outcome on what its adherents say is pervasive racism in the United States."[5]

CRT is taught in many high schools and universities, and was designed to ignite a cultural paradigm shift, moving from educational institutions into society, government and our personal lives. Troy and I see it as not just a theory but a dangerous philosophy that, if left unchecked, will radically alter the world. In fact, we see it as part of the movement toward a one-world government. (More on that shortly.)

Xi Van Fleet, a Chinese American woman who grew up in Communist China, believes that today's woke revolution, driven by CRT, has a "twin brother" in the Cultural Revolution under Chairman Mao. CRT creates false racial divisions, she says, actually redefining racism. It sees triggering chaos as a means to an end:

> It's the same tactic; it's Marx's tactic. So what they do is create chaos. As Mao said, "When the worst chaos emerges, that is when the greatest control can be achieved." They want to create chaos so that they [can] overthrow the existing system. . . . Cancel culture is the same because what the people [want to] do here is to overthrow the American founding [principles],

just like [in] China—to overthrow the traditional culture and our civilization.[6]

Ephesians 4:14 warns us not to be "blown here and there by every wind of teaching and by the cunning and craftiness of people in their deceitful scheming."

If you do not think that a philosophy can affect a culture, look at the demonic philosophy of Friedrich Nietzsche, whose concept of *Übermensch* ("Overman" or "Superman") as a goal for humanity influenced the Nazis to murder millions under Adolf Hitler. Nietzsche himself, according to Benjamin Wiker, was influenced by Charles Darwin and his theory of biological evolution—another philosophy that has undermined faith and altered the culture. Wiker, a senior fellow at the Discovery Institute's Center for Science and Culture, writes that

> Darwinism is responsible for a lot more destruction than the eugenic fantasies of the Third Reich. He can also claim substantial patrimony for the rantings of philosopher Friedrich Nietzsche that likewise inspired the intellectuals that surrounded and supported Hitler's scheme.
>
> Nietzsche is famous for declaring that "God is dead," and asserting in his infamous *Beyond Good and Evil*, that mere morality, like religion, is for cowering slaves. The future must belong to the real masters, proclaimed Nietzsche just before the horrors of the 20th century, to those who disregard moral limits, override distinctions between good and evil, and shedding charity for cruelty, impose their will on others for the sake of their own earthly glory.[7]

When we put on our night-vision goggles, we can discern what the Word of God says—about control, personal responsibility, anarchy, chaos, rejection of the Creator and so much more—in order to cut through the darkness and deception.

Black Lives Matter

As we are leaving on our NVGs, let's be clear. The important phrase *Black lives matter* is very true. Black lives *do* matter. But that name does not reflect the true nature of this organization. As The Heritage Foundation aptly puts it, "The agenda of Black Lives Matter is far different from the slogan."[8]

As with other far-left agendas, BLM is all about creating a Marxist government that leads to a New World Order.

A hinge point for the overthrow of the social order began in May 2020 when an African American man, George Floyd, was killed by a police officer in Minneapolis, Minnesota, after being suspected of passing a counterfeit twenty-dollar bill in a grocery store. The killing itself was reprehensible, and was followed by protests against racism and police brutality— then riots, looting and chaos, not only in Minneapolis but nationwide.

BLM and others began calling for defunding the police because of brutality against Blacks. To create anarchy in any culture, you must first unravel its social order. A statement made by the president of the Greater New York Black Lives Matter, Hank Newsome, was instructive:

> "If this country doesn't give us what we want, then we will burn down this system and replace it. All right? And I could be speaking figuratively. I could be speaking literally. It's a matter of interpretation."[9]

The BLM machine continues to profess that it is a peaceful, nonviolent movement that wants to do good for the Black community. But the following text on the Black Lives Matter website—taken down in September 2020 after public criticism by a former player in the National Football League (who is Black)—is revealing:

We disrupt the Western-prescribed nuclear family structure re-
quirement by supporting each other as extended families and
'villages' that collectively care for one another. . . .[10]

Troy and I see "[disrupting] the Western-prescribed nuclear
family structure" as part of BLM's intent to overthrow the
traditional family.

The co-founder of the BLM organization, Patrisse Cullors,
was mentored by Eric Mann, a leader in the 1960s in the
Weather Underground, described by the FBI as a domestic
terrorist group. Cullors was reportedly tutored for years in
Marxist-Leninist ideology and stated publicly that she is a
trained Marxist.[11] In May 2021 she resigned as executive director of Black Lives Matter under a cloud of questions over
the group's finances and her own lavish lifestyle, including the
purchase of four high-end homes.[12]

Is Black Lives Matter deceptive propaganda? Listen to this
Black columnist for *Townhall*, Elizabeth Matory:

We are being pushed off the proverbial cliff by the carefully
crafted BLM. The only solution is to not participate at all. Just
like other destructive propaganda in the past, society needs to
forcefully reject it. No good will ever come from destroying
property, burning and looting businesses, and shutting down
constructive dialogue. Solutions are not what the BLM movement wants. They want total destruction of society. And if you
are not OK with that and if you're not OK with the destructive
BLM movement, you're not a racist. You are a decent human
being who has found the truth.[13]

One-World Order

While I was a student at the U.S. Army War College in Carlisle,
Pennsylvania, almost every book I read stated that the only
way to attain world peace and stability was by having a world

government. It makes sense to the natural mind. Who does not want a stable and peaceful world?

We know by reading the Bible, however, that Satan will rule the nations through a man called the Antichrist. Satan will literally indwell or incarnate himself in this human being, just as he did with Judas Iscariot: "Satan entered Judas, the one called Iscariot, who belonged to the number of the twelve" (Luke 22:3).

Let's take a look behind the scenes of the growing movement toward a one-world order.

The Council on Foreign Relations (CFR) is a think tank focusing on U.S. foreign policy and international relations. It calls itself

> an independent, nonpartisan membership organization, think tank, and publisher dedicated to being a resource for its members, government officials, business executives, journalists, educators and students, civic and religious leaders, and other interested citizens in order to help them better understand the world and the foreign policy choices facing the United States and other countries.[14]

These are some nice-sounding words, right? Now let's put on our NVGs and look more closely.

The CFR was founded in 1921 in New York City with the main purpose of advising governments on international affairs. A who's who of major financiers, politicians, business executives, journalists, religious leaders and others have belonged to or now belong to the CFR, including among American politicians both Democrats and Republicans.

When President George H. W. Bush spoke of a "New World Order" on September 11, 1990, during the Persian Gulf crisis, he was referring to the mantra of the CFR.[15]

The CFR is an influential organization (one among many) working to bring about a world government as part of a one-world order. Despite its claim to the contrary, it is not independent or nonpartisan. It was connected to such notables as the Rockefellers and other influential families.

The founders, according to William F. Jasper in *The New American*, were the "architects of, and propagandists for, the failed League of Nations following World War I, as well as engineers of the successful effort that launched the United Nations after World War II." Jasper believes that the CFR wants "to build an all-powerful world government." He explains,

> Through both Democrat and Republican administrations, the CFR's members and minions have provided the leadership for the devastating programs and policies that are now dangerously close to extinguishing freedom as we know it and terminating our constitutional republic. They are, for example, the main promoters of, and cheerleaders for, open borders, unsustainable spending and taxing, foreign aid, LGBTQ "diversity," racial polarization and discord . . . gun confiscation, feminization and politicization of our military, fanatical environmentalism, global-warming hysteria, COVID panic . . . Big Tech censorship, oppressive regulation, trade policies that are outsourcing our industry and technology, communistic cancel culture, federal usurpation of state and local authority, indoctrination of our children and youth in immorality and Marxist ideology—and much, much more. [16]

Keeping Our Goggles On

Let's sum up with apt admonitions from two leaders.

As deception increases in the end times, according to Dr. Robert Jeffress,

> People will be open to any lie and any deception of Satan. I do believe that we're going to see these lies increase, and people who have rejected the absolute truth of God's Word are going

to be the prime targets and victims of this error. It will be pervasive through what I believe is going to be a very real one-world dictator known as the Antichrist. The Antichrist will be known for speaking blasphemies and lies. But they won't appear that way. He will entrance people with his charisma, but behind his smile are devious lies that will lead people astray. [17]

Jack Hibbs, senior pastor of the ten-thousand-member Calvary Chapel Chino Hills, told his congregation in Southern California,

Jesus said there will come a time of escalation of deception against the truth. He said 2,000 years ago that there will be an escalation of the deconstruction of society. . . . Jesus said there would come an escalation of calamities on earth. Just look at Matthew 24:7 for that Scripture. Jesus said there would be an escalation of the death of brotherly love, that man's common, general love for one another would grow cold (Matthew 24:10, 12). Jesus said there would be an escalation of the devaluing of human life (Luke 17:26). Ask yourself if these things are true right now. [18]

Yes. And it is essential to keep on our night-vision goggles.

TACTICS, TECHNIQUES AND PROCEDURES

1. **Ask God for discernment.** To put on your spiritual NVGs, ask God for "discerning of spirits," one of the spiritual gifts listed by the apostle Paul in 1 Corinthians 12: 7–11. This gift of the Holy Spirit allows believers to distinguish between the influence of God, Satan, the world and the

flesh in different situations. The Church needs those with this gift to warn believers of danger and to keep them from going astray because of false teaching.

2. **Read, read, read.** Do not accept at face value what the news is telling you. Much is misinformation, representing the bias of the source, or else actual propaganda. Find trusted sources and mature, godly mentors who will help you discern the times. Remember the sons of Issachar, "who understood the times and knew what Israel should do" (1 Chronicles 12:32).

3. **Determine to be a Daniel.** Daniel decided to obey God and not the king. His enemies reported that "Daniel, who is one of the exiles from Judah, pays no attention to you, Your Majesty, or to the decree you put in writing. He still prays three times a day" (Daniel 6:13). For his obedience to God, Daniel was thrown into a den of lions—but we know that story had a happy ending.

8

Politics and Media: Age of Deception

In my vision at night I looked, and there before me was one like a son of man, coming with the clouds of heaven. He approached the Ancient of Days and was led into his presence.

DANIEL 7:13

LATE 1980S
FORT CARSON, COLORADO, MECHANIZED INFANTRY
TRAINING, 7TH INFANTRY DIVISION
OVERCAST NIGHT

As my assistant and I drove through the night training exercise in Piñon Canyon, I discovered to my utter amazement that my GEN III night-vision goggles did not work when it is overcast and there is absolutely no starlight or moonlight.

NVGs work to pull in a fraction of light from the night sky and then magnify it so your eyes can see in the darkness—except in the case of total darkness. Then you are out of luck.

But even in the darkness of Babylon in the sixth century BC, the prophet Daniel had a night vision of the Lord Jesus Christ, who was presented before the Father, the Ancient of Days. Daniel was able to see through the thickest darkness because he had the light of God in him.

The Bible goes on to tell us that Daniel saw "one like a son of man"—Jesus Christ—

> given authority, glory and sovereign power; all nations and peoples of every language worshiped him. His dominion is an everlasting dominion that will not pass away, and his kingdom is one that will never be destroyed.
>
> Daniel 7:14

Daniel, who had this night vision of the Lord Jesus Christ, is considered one of the greatest of all prophets and is named by the Lord as one of His favorites (see Ezekiel 14:14–20). In Judaism Daniel is considered a sage, which is a level higher than the prophets, because of the wisdom with which God endowed him. With spiritual night-vision goggles, Daniel was able to see far into the future to the time in which we are now living, the end times.

Daniel was a man of high intellect and high position who (like the sons of Issachar in 1 Chronicles 12:32) understood the times he lived in. (We will look at Daniel in more detail in chapter 9.) Ancient Babylon was considered the greatest nation on earth. No one imagined she could be taken down in one night, but she was—as written in Daniel 5.

The fall of Babylon, late in the life of Daniel, was due to the excessive pride of her king, Belshazzar, the excesses of the sins of the people and the arrogance of the elite. King Belshazzar went so far as to take the holy vessels that had been carried to Babylon from the Temple in Jerusalem and use them in a party to toast their gods.

We are now living in the age of Babylon, an age of spectacular deception, propaganda, deceit, arrogance and dishonesty, especially in politics and the media.

In the 1944 classic film *Gaslight,* a murderer who has recently gotten married manipulates his wife into believing she is going insane to distract her from learning of his crimes. It is from this movie that emerged the term *gaslighting,* meaning using psychological manipulation to get someone to doubt his or her sanity.

Is it possible that believers today are being gaslighted by the political and media elites? Do you ever feel out of sync with the culture? Listen to David Kupelian in an article in *Whistleblower*:

> News flash: America's current ruling elites—including . . . Big Media, the "Deep State," academia, and even an increasing number of major "woke" corporations—are literally gaslighting the rest of America every single day, from morning until night, in a dizzying and ever-expanding variety of ways.
>
> Truly, gaslighting has become the No. 1 psychological-spiritual warfare principle of America's ruling class. The most obvious example of . . . gaslighting is [the] ongoing campaign to not only demonize but induce paralyzing doubt, guilt, fear and self-loathing in tens of millions of thoroughly decent, patriotic, law-abiding, conservative Americans by continually denouncing them as "racists," "white supremacists," "violent extremists" and "domestic terrorists." . . . As with all gaslighting, the intended effect here is to confuse, confound, distress, dispirit, intimidate and bewilder people to the point they doubt obvious truths they once knew and instead live in fear and anxiety, thus disabling them from being effective in the ongoing war for America's future.[1]

The mission of followers of Jesus is even more critical, and the ongoing war even more intense.

Politics: The New Religion

Prussian General Carl von Clausewitz stated that "war is nothing but a continuation of politics with the admixture of other means."[2] What von Clausewitz meant is that politics is the overarching principle by which we all live. Politics reflects the beliefs of those who are in power. But if those in power have a corrupt worldview and lifestyle, then it follows that their supporters (those who elected them) probably support and reflect that worldview and lifestyle as well.

Politics, for many, is the new religion of the 21st century. This religion has many requirements. To follow it, you are expected to bow at the altar of deception.

Yes, it is important to vote, to be involved in your community and to stay abreast of current affairs. But look at the leader as much as his or her platform. What does he or she actually believe and live?

Let's put on our NVGs and see what is happening behind the scenes in the darkness.

First and foremost, it is important to understand that politics cannot save you. Led by fallible human beings, politicians will always let you down. Remember, too, that politics and politicians come and go. "The grass withers and the flowers fall, but the word of our God endures forever" (Isaiah 40:8).

Next, understand that there is always an agenda behind politics and politicians. And behind the agenda stand forces of darkness that seek to control the narrative and the direction of that narrative. Part of the current narrative is the goal of world globalization. Whenever you hear about global warming, the great reset, the world economic condition or admonitions from the United Nations or the CFR, know that the ultimate goal is a one-world government.

Third, ask the Lord for eyes to see and ears to hear (see Matthew 13:15)—like the prophet Daniel—and not blindly believe all that is being said in the political world, on both the left and the right, so you will steer clear of deception. Political parties on both sides of the spectrum belong to many of the same globalization groups.

It is easy to get off the path God has for us, and politics can do that.

Jesus and Politics

In Luke 12:13–15, Jesus is asked to get involved in arbitrating between two brothers and their fight over an inheritance:

> Jesus replied, "Man, who appointed me a judge or an arbiter between you?" Then he said to them, "Watch out! Be on your guard against all kinds of greed; life does not consist in an abundance of possessions."

Jesus helps us with a key point here: Don't get sidetracked by the important versus the imperative. Yes, the inheritance was an important issue for the man asking Jesus for help; he may have needed it for personal goals or even his family's future. But Jesus cut to the chase by suggesting the danger of a sinful motive, and also by sticking to His own mission as the Son of God: "If I stop and chase down every important thing that comes My way, I will not have time for the imperative—that which the Father has commanded Me."

Another time, some religious leaders tried to test Jesus' loyalty to Rome:

> They came to him and said, "Teacher, we know that you are a man of integrity. You aren't swayed by others, because you pay no attention to who they are; but you teach the way of God in accordance with the truth. Is it right to pay the imperial tax to Caesar or not? Should we pay or shouldn't we?"
> But Jesus knew their hypocrisy. "Why are you trying to trap me?" he asked. "Bring me a denarius and let me look at it."

111

They brought the coin, and he asked them, "Whose image is this? And whose inscription?"

"Caesar's," they replied.

Then Jesus said to them, "Give back to Caesar what is Caesar's and to God what is God's."

And they were amazed at him.

Mark 12:14–17

Jesus never allowed anyone to coerce Him to go another route than what the Father had planned. Yes, there are those whom God has ordained to go the political route, but politics can get us off God's path. We all need to be careful not to get sidetracked by political deception.

Politics and the Antichrist

The Antichrist, as we have seen, will be both a religious and a political leader. The Bible identifies him by various names, including "the man of sin" and "the son of perdition" (2 Thessalonians 2:3 NKJV), "the beast" (Revelation 13; 19:19–20) and the Antichrist (1 John 2:18). He will convince the world to follow him because he will claim to be God, as evidenced by the miracles he will perform. People will be mesmerized and think he is the Christ, the Messiah, because of his miracles, leadership, political appeal, personal appeal and a host of other attractive qualities.

At first the Antichrist will seem like "a benevolent leader who is universally loved and adored," writes Dr. Thomas R. Horn, a bestselling prophecy author and chief executive officer of SkyWatch TV, and his co-author Terry James, in *Antichrist and the Final Solution*. The global government of this leader will not be "perceived as a dictatorship deadlier than all preceding despotic regimes." On the other hand, write Horn and James:

He'll have his own Final Solution in bringing his satanically controlled regime into being. He is a "beast," according to God's

Word. That is, he will have a beastly nature—like Hitler, Stalin, Mao, and the others. But Antichrist will be much, much more powerful—more deadly than they were. He will have his own version of Hitler's propaganda minister Josef Goebbels. This False Prophet is called the "second beast." He will force everyone to worship the image of Antichrist. . . .

We can see, as we look around the geopolitical, socioeconomic, and religious landscape of the hour, the stage is being set for the rise of the Antichrist. His Final Solution is being prepared even now for all those who inhabit this earthly sphere when he steps upon the stage to rule during the final years of earth's history leading up to Christ's Second Advent.[3]

Media: The Propaganda Machine

Author, poet and ex-criminal lawyer Robert Black once said: "In dictatorships the media is controlled by the State. In democracies the media is controlled by wealthy individuals with political affiliations. Objective media and journalists simply do not exist in the mainstream."[4]

I had an instructive experience with the media while I was at Fort Campbell, Kentucky, in 2002.

One morning I was driving to work after physical training (PT) to provide needed counseling to soldiers of the 101st Airborne Division. As I entered the main gate on my way to the Family Life Center, I got a phone call from my boss, the installation chaplain. He told me to meet him at the main post chapel. As I drove into the parking lot, I was overwhelmed at the number of vehicles crammed into that small lot. And as I entered the chapel, I discovered the reason: It was full of news reporters, cameras and commotion.

My boss, who was at the front, signaled me to come forward so the press could ask me questions about the departure of the 101st and the family members left behind. About fifty microphones were shoved in front of me as the press peppered me with questions. And later my boss set me up with a reporter from a national newspaper. We spent about an hour doing an interview.

And the next day I was appalled to see myself on the front page with a quote taken way out of context.

Then the spouse of the division commander walked up to me with that newspaper in hand, waving it angrily. How, she asked me, could I have said such a thing? I assured her that I had not. And when I reminded her how many times her husband had been misquoted as well, she calmed down.

As I say, that experience was instructive.

It is no secret that the mass media is one of the least trusted groups in America. Statista, a German-based market leader of business data across 170 industries and 150-plus countries, states that in the United States only 29 percent of adults trust the news most of the time.[5]

The press is a propaganda machine paid for by the elite to get their message out to America and the world. They make big money to get us to hate one side or the other, according to a brilliant reporter, Matt Taibbi, in the *Washington Spectator*:

> Accept a binary world and pick a side. Embrace the reality of being surrounded by evil stupidity. Feel indignant, righteous, and smart. Hate losers, love winners. Don't challenge yourself. And during the commercials, do some shopping.[6]

Troy and I believe that the world is being set up through various propaganda machines for the end times. If our enemy, Satan, can get us to focus on all the hatred and divide us, he can keep us from seeing what is really going on in the world. This is an old military tactic of deception.

When you study the rise of Nazi Germany in the 1930s and its use of propaganda to influence its citizens, the similarities to modern-day news outlets are striking. Adolf Hitler had a massive propaganda machine—using newspapers, radio, film and more—to indoctrinate Germany in Nazi ideology, especially anti-Semitism. The Nazis were able to use deception to stir hatred of the Jews to such a point that they were exterminated in concentration camps by the millions.

As it was in the days of Germany's Third Reich, so it shall be in these end times. Dr. Robert Jeffress says he is very concerned that many Christians are being manipulated by the media.

> I tell my people, if you're anxious all the time and upset and angry, watch less television, look at fewer websites, listen to less talk radio. I can tell you from personal experience, it doesn't matter what network we're talking about, they have one goal, and that is to get as many eyeballs as they can watching—and they know how to do it. When they have their story meetings every morning, they say, "What can we do to make our audience either anxious or angry?" That's what their goal is because they know what attracts eyeballs and gets dollars.
>
> Don't be a victim of the media. We should take our cues from God's Word.[7]

Be careful, then, where you get your information. Recognize the propaganda in media, politics, education, even in the Church. If your news source is a constant diet of mainstream media, you may be in big trouble in your thoughts and personal life. Be vigilant about what you watch, read and listen to. Measure every thought and idea against the touchstone of God's Word.

The Belt of Truth

Soldiers of the Roman legions in the first century and beyond wore the *cingulum militare* or *balteus*, the traditional military belt. The purpose of the belt was to hold weapons in place, such as swords, spears and knives, as well as to keep the soldier's tunic and other clothing tucked in. According to Romans in Britain, a historical website:

> The balteus is a mark of a soldier—not only that, it's really a status symbol of being a soldier. Worn at all times, even off duty, only soldiers were allowed, by law, to wear this unique belt. It may have had some defensive capabilities. . . . The archaeological evidence suggests that many of these belts were intricately elaborate.[8]

Like the Roman soldiers, followers of Christ must put on the belt of truth: "Stand firm then, with the belt of truth buckled around your waist" (Ephesians 6:14). The belt of truth holds us together from the onslaught of deception. The truth is none other than the Word of God.

The problem right now is that many believers do not see the Word of God as absolute truth, which is a lie from Satan. If you live according to your own feelings, or the beliefs of the culture around you, you will surely fall into deception.

If Scripture is not the inerrant Word of God, then people can believe or not believe what they choose, and exercise the ability to do "whatever [seems] right in their own eyes" (Judges 21:25 NLT). The great Church Reformers identified a principle that the Church should never forget: *sola scriptura*, which means "by Scripture alone." *Sola scriptura* recognizes the fact that the Word of God is the infallible source of authority for Christian faith and practice.

Greater than a leader like Martin Luther—who was the catalyst for the sixteenth-century Protestant Reformation and one of the most influential figures in the history of Christianity—the Bible declares *itself* to be the authority for the believer, inspired by the Holy Spirit, the very Word of God:

> No prophecy of Scripture came about by the prophet's own interpretation of things. For prophecy never had its origin in

the human will, but prophets, though human, spoke from God as they were carried along by the Holy Spirit.

2 Peter 1:20–21

All Scripture is God-breathed and is useful for teaching, rebuking, correcting and training in righteousness.

2 Timothy 3:16

Let's pray for vision, clarity and wisdom to discern the times. And to avoid being deceived, and to fulfill our calling as soldiers of the King's army, we must buckle on God's Word as the belt of truth every day.

TACTICS, TECHNIQUES AND PROCEDURES

1. **Practice speaking the truth.** Once you have asked God for discernment (one of the "Tactics, Techniques and Procedures" in the last chapter), speak the truth of God's Word every day against the false messages of politics and media. When you read a headline that you know is not true, or hear a political leader spin the truth wrongly, declare the truth out loud and use applicable Scriptures.

2. **Make sure your pastor preaches the Word of God.** Be sure your pastor and other favorite leaders teach the "whole counsel of God" (Acts 20:27 NKJV) and every aspect of the Gospel of Jesus Christ, not just favorite topics.

3. **Put on the belt of truth.** God's Word defies political and media propaganda, false narratives and cancel culture. Meditate on the Word of God, allow the Holy Spirit to speak to you, and act on what the Word is telling you to do.

9

Education: Indoctrination and Propaganda

In war, the way is to avoid what is strong, and strike at what is weak.

SUN TZU

2012
U.S. ARMY WAR COLLEGE, CARLISLE BARRACKS
CARLISLE, PENNSYLVANIA

The Army has sent me to be educated as a field grade officer to work at the higher levels of the military. Commanding generals expect their staffs to be educated in the Army at the strategic level.

So the Army has brought me and many other officers to the War College to make us better, more decisive leaders and strategists—not just educated but well-rounded, knowledgeable and decisive. The one word pounded into us day after day is *strategy*. The Army wants us to be strategic thinkers.

And one thing I discover in my coursework at the War College (as I have indicated) is that many books and leaders are advocating a one-world government to end humankind's power struggle. After all, they say, if the world had one government, then wars would be eliminated.

Or so they think.

Strategic thinking includes being able to see the entire picture from start to end, the whole "battlespace" where the enemy can strike from space, air, land and sea, as well as via digital and electronic forms of warfare. (We will talk more about battlespace in chapter 13.)

Our heavenly Father wants all His children to become strategic thinkers, educated with a biblical worldview, having renewed minds, familiar with the teaching of the prophets who predicted all that is happening today, and following the "whole counsel of God."

The U.S. Army spends tens of millions of dollars each year on training and education, recognizing its vital importance. Training and Doctrine Command (TRADOC) is the Army headquarters responsible for training and education in the Army. TRADOC produces all Army field and training manuals, as well as all literature pertaining to education. My entire career was built on being educated in the Army's way of doing things, from basic training as a second lieutenant all the way to the War College, promoted to colonel.

TRADOC is to the Army what home and church are to the believer. At home and at church are the primary places where believers are trained in biblical truth as disciples of Jesus. Seminaries train pastors and pastors train believers. Pastors who take their work seriously understand their responsibility "for the equipping of the saints for the work of ministry" (Ephesians 4:12).

In the epigraph at the beginning of this chapter, Sun Tzu, the great ancient Chinese war strategist, encouraged military leaders to strike at what is weak, not what is strong. He was not an advocate of frontal assault, going headfirst into the teeth of an enemy's stronghold and getting wiped out. His was a strategy of stealth, cunning and wisdom in war.

In the same way, our enemy, Satan, knows full well that the slow erosion of morals, the constant attack on education through moral relativism and the continuous assault on the Bible and the Church will win the day and bring about the rise of the Antichrist and a world government. That is the way of deception.

The Power of Education

Dictators, fascists, Communists, socialists and other totalitarian rulers understand very well the power of education. That is why, in every revolution to overthrow stable government, the first ones to go are educated people.

Former Soviet Union dictator Joseph Stalin, in the Great Purge of 1936–38, had at least 750,000 people executed, including members of his own party, educated people, dissidents and anyone else he considered a threat to his power. More than a million more were sent off to forced labor camps, known as gulags.[1]

Martin Latsis, chief of the Ukrainian secret police organization Cheka in 1919, stated in the newspaper *Red Terror*,

> We are not fighting against single individuals. We are exterminating the bourgeoisie as a class. Do not look in materials you have gathered for evidence that a suspect acted or spoke against the Soviet authorities. The first question you should ask him is what class he belongs to, what is his origin, education, profession. These questions should determine his fate. This is the essence of the Red Terror.[2]

Satan knows the power of education and that the key in bringing the world to its knees is educating the masses with his doctrines of socialism, Communism and every other "ism" out there that subverts the cause of Christ.

Coaches in baseball and other sports know that the best way to field a team and get the best players is to start training in the elementary schools and grow their teams all the way up to college and then professional sports. So it goes in education.

Mary Ann Peluso McGahan, a minister, conference speaker, television host and gospel music singer who worked closely with David Wilkerson at Times Square Church in New York City, comments on the pervasiveness of Marxist indoctrination and deceptive ideologies taught to young people in public schools, colleges and universities:

> In the educational system there has been a plan set in order for decades now involving an Antichrist system of indoctrination. The evolution of situational ethics and critical race theory is huge. Deception comes in early in the elementary schools as the colleges are churning out teachers who in turn are going back with these ideologies to other educational institutions.
>
> Evolution, which says there is no God, and situational ethics—in other words, you make up ethics for whatever situation you want—result in lawlessness. Critical race theory is not love. Everybody is against a certain population, and that breeds division. I see that being paralleled in the Church. I see the enemy speaking to many Christians, who are being deceived because they make up a situation and then pull a Scripture that will fit that ethic.[3]

Navigating "Reeducation"

The life of the prophet Daniel becomes very important to us now. He was taken from his home as part of the royal family in Jerusalem and brought to serve King Nebuchadnezzar in Babylon, who had conquered Judah.

121

The king wanted to assimilate the best young men of Jerusalem into his kingdom, so he commanded that those of royal descent in Judah be "reeducated" and trained so they would forget their heritage and learn the ways of Babylon. The story is found in Daniel 1:3–5:

> The king ordered Ashpenaz, chief of his court officials, to bring into the king's service some of the Israelites from the royal family and the nobility—young men without any physical defect, handsome, showing aptitude for every kind of learning, well informed, quick to understand, and qualified to serve in the king's palace. He was to teach them the language and literature of the Babylonians. The king assigned them a daily amount of food and wine from the king's table. They were to be trained for three years, and after that they were to enter the king's service.

The king knew that to make ready royal subjects, they would have to be "reeducated." Anytime kings or dictators want to change society, they start with a reeducation program, much like the Communists in Russia and China. The three-year reeducation process in Babylon included giving the Jewish exiles new names, clothes, food and literature, and teaching them the new language.

So Daniel found himself in a foreign land with pagan gods and a very different set of rules. But he "resolved not to defile himself with the royal food and wine" (Daniel 1:8), thus resisting the defilement of Babylon. He posed an experiment to the chief official for himself and his three Hebrew friends that they eat only vegetables, and the official could see how they fared. They flourished, were allowed this diet and thus resisted compromise with the pagan nation.

In the same way, we must take a stand against the rising tide of systematic reeducation by those whose purpose is to bring about a global network of nations.

"I think we can learn a lot from the prophet Daniel," says McGahan, former associate of David Wilkerson. She believes that the Body of Christ is in a critical place, a place of soul-searching and getting our houses in order:

> Daniel set himself apart. He did not consume the royal food and wine. It will take a real commitment in this hour for us to say, "I'm going to stand up and not participate. I'm not going to eat the king's delicacies." When we position ourselves like that, there's going to be a boldness, a strength, an ability to stand up against the Antichrist spirit.
>
> Daniel 7:25 says the man of sin, the Antichrist, will try "to change times and laws." We're in a place right now that calls for radical Christianity, as this Antichrist spirit is coming on the scene in the schools and trying to shut down churches. So there's got to be radical commitment to Christ.
>
> God will raise people up to set a new standard and prepare the way for a great revival, even as God preserved Daniel. God will preserve His people in this hour and use them in a mighty way for one last great revival and harvest.[4]

Encroaching Progressivism

In an article in the *Washington Times*, Matt Bennett points out that America's most prestigious Ivy League colleges—Harvard, Princeton and Yale—were founded as Christian institutions by faith leaders. He writes,

> The Bible was once highly valued in the curriculum of the first universities founded in America. Harvard's original motto which can be seen in the front room on the third floor of the Harvard Club in New York was "Veritas pro Christo et pro ecclesiae" (Truth for Christ and the Church). Yale's motto is "Lux et Veritas" (Light and Truth). Up until the 19th century, knowing Hebrew and ancient Greek was essential to get into Harvard founded in 1636 and Yale founded in 1701.[5]

Over time, however, progressive liberalism and moral relativism crept into the vaunted universities and educational systems of America. Charles Eliot, president of Harvard in 1869, selected Christopher Langdell as the first dean of Harvard Law School in 1870. Matt Bennett describes the changes that occurred:

> Langdell removed Sir William Blackstone Commentaries on the Laws of England which had been the standard teaching text in Law Schools. Blackstone (1723–1780) was a recognized legal English scholar who believed that the Ten Commandments should be at the heart of his Commentaries. He believed that mankind was created by God and granted rights by God. Man's law must be based on God's law, which was the basic concept in the Declaration of Independence. Dean Langdell reversed Blackstone's belief in the supremacy of God's law by teaching man's law as supreme when he introduced the case study method of law. Case law introduced the notion of moral relativism into the study of law instead of the prior absolutes in law. Starting in 1890, other law schools started to follow the case study method, which has become standard teaching.[6]

Deception does not usually take hold quickly; its insidious work may come over decades or even longer. The fruits we are seeing today are the result of many years of planting dangerous seeds. Eliot and Langdell were succumbing to the pressures of businessmen of the day who wanted a "practical" education for their sons that did not include the Bible or the classical literature of Europe.

Today's higher educational systems, including colleges, universities and even seminaries, are rife with progressive administrators and professors who promote socialist, Marxist and globalist ideals that permeate churches, businesses and schools. Many universities will not hire conservative or Christian professors who espouse a different worldview. Many schools actually squelch free speech from outside speakers, or even among their own faculty and student bodies, that reflect a conservative or faith point of view.

John Dewey, an educational reformer born in 1859 who taught at the University of Chicago and Columbia University, spearheaded the progressive movement in education. Education, he stated, must bring about a "new social order." As a result, progressive education "now has more than 85 percent of American children in its grip."[7]

For this to have happened, and for there to be a new social order, the Bible could not remain the cornerstone of the educational system. Sure enough, in June 1963 the U.S. Supreme Court, whose members were educated in the very Ivy League schools that were established as religious institutions, ruled 8–1 that "officially mandated" Bible reading and prayer in public schools is unconstitutional. Such practices, according to the court, violate the establishment clause of the First Amendment, which prohibits Congress from making any law "respecting an establishment of religion." This ruling effectively removed God from public schools and profoundly changed the understanding of separation of Church and state.[8]

Alex Newman, senior editor at the *New American* magazine, executive director of Public School Exit and co-author of *Crimes of the Educators: How Utopians Are Using Government Schools to Destroy America's Children*, believes that the founding fathers of America's educational system wanted to turn America into a Communist nation:

Dewey went to the (former) Soviet Union and loved what they were doing, and said so publicly. He said their educational system is great; it's instilling a collectivist mentality into the children. He wanted to spread the false religion he called humanism. He was one of the original co-authors and signers of *The Humanist Manifesto.*

His religion was basically Communism. It was the same lie from the pit of hell that Satan used on Eve: "Did God really say? God just knows that if you disobey, then you'll be like God and you'll know good and evil for yourself." It's the same lie that the humanists are selling to our children under the leadership of John Dewey through the public school system to this day—the idea that there is no God, that man can be his own little god, that we can decide for ourselves what's right and wrong. It is diabolical.[9]

Countering Satan's Plan

There are many schoolteachers, including Christian teachers, who have not signed on to this lie. But the goal of an elite group of progressive educators is, first and foremost, to turn our children away from Christ, and then to turn them away from the concepts God has instituted for our benefit—marriage, family, private property, nation-states and the system of morality God lays out clearly in the Bible.

How is it going? Newman says,

They have done a phenomenal job. They have de-Christianized the United States and Europe remarkably quickly. A civilization that took thousands of years to build has been fundamentally transformed in a period of a few generations, and it was through the government school system that this was accomplished.

Now there is a new and improved version of this with the great reset that they're moving online. They hope to facilitate this transformation even more quickly than before through data gathering, monitoring and advanced psychological and behavioral psychology techniques to change the way children think. But the objective is the same: to turn us away from God, turn us away from our families, turn us away from our country, and turn us toward the New World Order that they're so fond of talking about in public these days.[10]

What to do? Newman has a strong view about how Christian parents handle primary and secondary education:

> I'd say, thing one, get your kids out of public schools. Thing two, get your children out of public schools. Thing three, get your children out of public schools. It's absolutely imperative; it's not optional. It's not like, "Well, maybe once our finances improve." You wouldn't leave your child in a burning building for obvious reasons, and you shouldn't leave your child in a government school for even more obvious reasons. A fire will hurt them physically; government schools are destroying them physically, mentally, emotionally, spiritually, academically, you name it.
>
> Once you've done the right thing in taking your children out, you've got to think, "Well, now what do I do?" I'd recommend finding some good homeschool resources and curriculums. I really think homeschooling is the gold standard. As I read the Bible, it's clear to me that God intended for parents to oversee the education and disciplining of their children.
>
> If you can't homeschool, you may want to try to find a good Christian school, affiliated with a church whose views you agree with.
>
> But the most important thing you can do for your children and for your country is to get them out of the government's brainwash camps and make sure they get a good, God-centered education.[11]

For higher education, many Christian teenagers have left home to attend a public college or university, only to return as unbelievers, atheists, socialists, Marxists or something else. A Pew Research Center survey released in December 2021 found that 29 percent of American adults have no religious affiliation, an increase of 6 percent from 2016, with millennials leading the shift away from faith.[12]

Parents need to be aware of what is being taught to their children and decide where to send their kids for higher education in these end times. I attended a secular university right out of high school. Yes, I encountered many godless professors. I thank God I was given the strength and ability to be a witness to many lost souls on campus. That doesn't mean it was good for me. Many believers were not strong and their faith became a shipwreck.

There are some great Christian schools and colleges, as well as campus groups that are in the fight and supporting students by teaching them the Gospel.

Satan's plan, as we have noted, is to bring all the nations under his sway and disrupt the plan of God for the return of His Son. Ultimately Satan will lose, but the fight continues.

What is your part? To understand the battle and to take a stand by proclaiming the truth of the Gospel, telling this truth to your pastor and publicly denouncing the Antichrist spirit in the educational system. And by reading the Bible and renewing your mind with a biblical worldview (see Romans 12:2).

Biblical education is a powerful force. In fact, Troy and I call upon all churches to reinstate Sunday school as well as midweek Bible studies!

TACTICS, TECHNIQUES AND PROCEDURES

1. **Take a stand for Christ.** Determine to take a stand for Jesus Christ in these end times by understanding what is being taught in public school from elementary school through college. We understand that, for financial or other pressing reasons, not everyone can take their children out of public school. But do look into alternate forms of education, like a private school, a charter school, a micro-school, online

learning or homeschooling; one of these options may be better for your family.

2. **Become your child's educator at home.** Don't let the government dictate to your kids what they need to learn; become their educator at home. Also, get your children into Sunday school and/or a Bible study.

3. **Consider joining the PTA.** Consider joining your school's Parent-Teacher Association (PTA). We know time is limited, but your investment as a Christian parent is invaluable and you will not fall into deception concerning your children.

4. **Read and teach the Bible at home,** every day, in the time you have available. God's Word will transform your life, and the lives of your family members, in profound ways.

10

Intellectual Deception: Technology, Evolution and UFOs

God is the name people give to the reason we are here. But I think that reason is the laws of physics rather than someone with whom one can have a personal relationship. An impersonal God.

STEPHEN HAWKING, theoretical physicist, cosmologist and author, *A Brief History of Time*

EARLY 1991
DHAHRAN AIR BASE, SAUDI ARABIA, TACTICAL
OPERATIONS CENTER (TOC)
NIGHT

I step into the TOC (housed in a military building) in the middle of the night to find myself surrounded with what we call "Star Wars technology and equipment" that is interfacing with the unit I am assigned: 1–43 Air Defense Artillery Patriot Battalion out of Fort Bliss, Texas. I deployed with 1–43 ADA to

Saudi Arabia. This unit is designed to shoot down any airborne threats such as aircraft and rockets.

My eyes adjust to the many lights on the scopes and screens linked to surrounding craft in space, air and sea. I stand amazed at the sophistication in technology and communication of our military.

Even now I cannot write about all the highly classified information I was hearing and seeing.

The U.S. military learned long ago that if it did not keep ahead in technology, then we would certainly lose the next war.

A little-known fact is that our technology has long been ahead of our tactics; that is the reason so many died in World War I. Soldiers were deploying using Napoleonic tactics from the previous wars in Europe (marching in rank and column) against the might of the newest technical marvels, the machine gun and advanced artillery. Hordes of soldiers on both sides, British and German, rushed headlong into waiting machine gun nests and were obliterated. It was called a frontal assault—not a smart idea against a weapon (the British Vickers and German *Maschinengewehr*) that could spew out more than six hundred rounds a minute.

So the first few months of World War I caused profound shock due to the huge casualties caused by these modern weapons, with one million men killed.[1] The Great War ended simply because both sides were out of gas and tired of the carnage with a total of 37 million causalities, including 8.5 million dead, 21 million wounded and 8 million prisoners of war or missing in action.[2]

The technological advances of weapons in the last 150 years, then, and the lagging behind of corresponding tactics proved a huge problem for the military.

In the same way, technology is one of three areas in particular—along with evolution and UFOs—that can set us up for deception. Let's take a closer look.

DECEPTION IN THE WORLD SYSTEM

The Deception of Technology

We think somehow that technology will save us from ourselves, build a better world, create a place of unity and foster health in our dying bodies.

Instead, our reliance on technology has created anxiety, stress, frustration and chaos. The illusion is that if only we had better technology, it would be a much better world. What many do not realize is that the ones who wield the powers of technology are the ones who will dominate the planet. Sometimes our greatest strength becomes our greatest weakness.

The invention of the car enabled people to travel quickly across town. It has also created enormous traffic jams, pollution and death. Nuclear power can be used to power up entire cities. It can also be used to destroy them. Computers help us in our work, economy and calculations, but they can also be used to track and monitor us around the globe, as they do in China.

Social Credit Scores

China is expanding a "social credit" system already in place that monitors behavior, scores it and doles out punishments and rewards accordingly, in an egregious violation of personal privacy and suppression of dissent, ostensibly to improve behavior and promote traditional values.

This social credit system punishes undesirable behavior with slowed internet speeds or travel bans for the citizens the Communist Party decides are untrustworthy.[3] In recent years China has spent billions of dollars to buy facial recognition, artificial intelligence and other digital technologies to add to its network of monitoring systems. Experts predict the nation could have as many as 300 million cameras installed soon to monitor citizens.[4]

According to the *New York Times*, eighteen countries—including Zimbabwe, Uzbekistan, Pakistan, Kenya, the United Arab Emirates and Germany—are using Chinese-made intelligent monitoring systems; and three dozen countries have received training in topics like "public opinion guidance," a euphemism for censorship.[5]

Alex Newman, the award-winning international journalist and author, says the "social credit system is not coming to America, it's here":

> It's been here for a while; they just haven't formally announced it. They have so much data on you, especially when you combine it with social media platforms. And make no mistake, all these Big Tech companies that you think are private companies—they're not. They were started with tax money and backing from the intelligence community and the military-industrial complex.
>
> So what's happening in China with social credit scores? Basically they wanted to find a way where they wouldn't always have to resort to brute force and absolute terror to keep people in line. They would much prefer if the slaves just obediently did what they're told without having to terrorize, kidnap, murder and torture them.[6]

With this goal in view, then, China's social credit score system has done marvels, because the Chinese people know if they criticize the government—or even if they have friends on social media who criticize the regime—they may not be able to travel, enroll their children in quality schools, obtain a mortgage or get a good job. So most just fall in line. Newman continues:

> That same system is now going global. Communist China was just the petri dish, the test market, but you can be sure that it will be formally unveiled in the days to come. We already have legislation introduced for the government to take over the credit rating system. The International Monetary Fund is talking about using your search engine searches to help determine your credit score.

All this data is being collated, analyzed and processed through artificial intelligence to make sense of it, and it will be used against you. I think you need to resist it actively anywhere you can. I've been giving them bad data for years. There's no reason why social media companies should have your real birthday. There's no reason they should know what city you live in or what religion you are. Honestly, it's not coming; it's here.[7]

This technology, made vastly more sophisticated, will one day be used around the globe by the world government headed by the Antichrist and the false prophet. Alex Newman says, "Be prepared and realize that there is going to be a cost for standing against evil."[8]

Technological Dependence

Advancements in technology can be a wonderful thing. Most of us have smartphones we depend on. But too often sophisticated technology leads to overdependence and vulnerability. If we were hit with an electromagnetic pulse (EMP) weapon like ones that North Korea, Russia and China possess, it could take out our entire electric grid with the loss of computers, power, water, transportation (including cars, trains and airplanes), the economy and a whole range of services on which we depend.

In addition, studies reveal a plethora of problems associated with our dependence on technology, including addiction to social media, loss of personal relationships, depression, anxiety, loneliness and many other issues. Many tell us that technology is the way ahead and the answer for the ills of society. The Bible tells us there is only one answer, and His name is Jesus Christ. But our world touts science as the key to all our problems.

Often coupled with that deception is the idea that there is no God, no divine being.

Atheists and God

Many scientists are atheists simply because they cannot prove that there is a God or conduct any scientific experiment to verify the existence of divinity. In this chapter about intellectual deception, let's look at two well-known scientists to learn what they believe about God and about life.

Richard Dawkins, evolutionary biologist and emeritus fellow of Oxford, wrote the following in his bestseller *The God Delusion*: "We are all atheists about most of the gods that humanity has ever believed in. Some of us just go one god further."[9]

Stephen Hawking, world-renowned theoretical physicist and cosmologist connected with Cambridge, was arguably one of the greatest minds on the planet. But he said,

I regard the brain as a computer which will stop working when its components fail. There is no heaven or afterlife for broken-down computers; that is a fairy story for people afraid of the dark.[10]

He also wrote in *The Grand Design*,

Because there is a law such as gravity, the universe can and will create itself from nothing. Spontaneous creation is the reason there is something rather than nothing, why the universe exists, why we exist. It is not necessary to invoke God to light the blue touch paper and set the universe going.[11]

Common sense tells us that the universe creating itself from nothing is preposterous. Hebrews 11:3 (ESV) says, "By faith we understand that the universe was created by the word of God, so that what is seen was not made out of things that are visible." And Romans 1:20 (ESV) makes the most eloquent and convincing argument that God created the universe and life:

For his invisible attributes, namely, his eternal power and divine nature, have been clearly perceived, ever since the creation of

135

the world, in the things that have been made. So [people] are without excuse.

The chief tactic of our enemy, and the underlying premise to all who would oppose Jesus Christ, is to lay the groundwork with seeds of unbelief and lies. It is subtle and deadly. Yet it is like a pandemic. You cannot see it, and when you do it may be too late.

The Deception of Evolution

"Were you there?" asks Ken Ham, the CEO and founder of Answers in Genesis and the Ark Encounter—meaning, Were you there when the big bang took place or when God created life?[12]

Charles Darwin published his book *On the Origin of Species* in 1859, proposing that all species developed from a common ancestor through the process of natural selection. The theory of evolution is so widely accepted today that it is now called the "science" of evolution. Science has progressed in a multitude of ways. Yet proof of evolution has lagged. We believe many universities and colleges are not being honest with their students when it comes to science and evolution.

But if the theory of evolution is debunked, then science is left with a big question: How did we get here?

Even so, scorn is heaped on those who would question or challenge the theory. Creationists and those who believe in intelligent design are routinely ridiculed—a tactic used by those who want to silence objections or suppress the truth.

Evolution as Religion

The core issue for most who believe in Darwin's theory of evolution is that if it is proven untrue, what is the alternative? The answer is a creative intelligence or Designer behind all of creation. The idea of intelligent design upends the entire nontheistic or secular worldview. If there is a Designer, then human beings as a species are responsible for our actions.

But it is convenient for evolutionists (not to say anyone!) *not* to believe in God, to live however they want and to be answerable to no higher authority. That is one of the main reasons they defend evolution with such passion: The alternative for them is not viable.

But Psalm 14:1 clearly states that "the fool says in his heart, 'There is no God.' They are corrupt, their deeds are vile; there is no one who does good."

David Hillel Gelernter, professor of computer science at Yale University, states that "Darwinism is no longer just a scientific theory but a basis of a worldview, and an emergency . . . religion for the many troubled souls who need one."[13]

Answering the Theory

Challenges to the theory of evolution proliferate.

Hugh Ross, founder and president of Reasons to Believe, is a prolific author and an astrophysicist with a Ph.D. in astronomy from the University of Toronto. He has spoken at hundreds of university campuses as well as conferences and churches around the world. Drawing on peer-reviewed literature, he says:

Many in the scientific community are becoming aware of just how improbable it is to explain the origin and history of life from the strictly naturalist perspective. In my book *Improbable Planet*, I cite five leading evolutionary biologists who have made this particular concession concerning the Cambrian explosion. And with every year that goes by, we find the scientific evidence growing in favor of supernatural intervention to explain the origin of life.

We personally go to conferences where these issues are being debated, where we've come to realize that many evolutionary biologists are "default atheists." They identify themselves as atheists, but they admit they've never really looked at the whole issue. When they meet scientists who have high integrity and credibility who believe in God, they're intrigued, and some want to talk. We've had marvelous conversations with some of the leading origin-of-life researchers and evolutionary biologists.[14]

Fazale Rana, vice president of research and apologetics at Reasons to Believe, writes about recent scientific discoveries regarding the mind-boggling complexities of DNA and cells and their implications:

> Advances in our understanding of biochemical systems revitalize William Paley's watchmaker argument for God's existence. The remarkable similarities between the architecture and operation of biochemical systems and human designs indicate that the cell's chemical systems are the work of a Mind. This observation also suggests that a resonance exists between the mind of human designers and the Intelligent Designer. To put it another way, human beings appear to be made in the image of the Intelligent Designer (Genesis 1:26–27).[15]

Parents and caretakers of teens going into secular and some religious universities need to prepare them (as we suggested at the end of the previous chapter) for the challenges they will face. Many teens growing up in Christian homes, unprepared for the secular onslaught in higher education, succumb to the nonreligionist or atheistic worldview of Darwinian evolution. Preparing for higher education must happen not only at home but at church as well.

Parents need to strongly consider with their teens the school choices available and ask, Is my child's eternal life worth more than a good-paying job and graduating from a prestigious school? Jesus posed this eternal question: "What good will it be for someone to gain the whole world, yet forfeit their soul?" (Matthew 16:26).

Hugh Ross points out that many parents today tend to release their responsibilities to educate their children to public schools and colleges:

> After all, we're busy. But we need to realize that we parents are responsible to train our children, to educate our children, to take a role in their education, and to equip them in critical thinking. I was educated at a time when critical thinking was part of the public school curriculum.
>
> I understand that's really rare right now; and so, given that it's not happening in public schools, and not even at the university level, with some exceptions, we need to take a major role in training our children to think critically, to recognize fallacies, and to engage in inductive reasoning—which means, of course, that we as parents need to be well equipped ourselves.[16]

The Deception of UFOs

One of the greatest sights I have ever seen on the battlefield was in Saudi Arabia after Desert Storm in 1991.

I have always been fascinated with outer space, the deep unknown and what is out there on other planets and in other galaxies. But one breathtaking night I was out in the Saudi desert, and the stars looked like a never-ending blanket of lights. My assistant and I were dumbfounded by the experience.

I am not the only one interested. There are too many sightings, encounters, government cover-ups and other unexplainable phenomena circulating to consider Unidentified Flying Objects (UFOs) a conspiracy theory anymore. What used to be considered fringe or extreme has become mainstream. UFOs are undoubtedly real.

But the question remains: What exactly are they?

In June 2021, for the first time since Project Blue Book—a systematic study of UFOs by the U.S. Air Force in 1969—the

U.S. government issued a new report. The Office of the Director of National Intelligence released its report on recent Unidentified Aerial Phenomena (UAP)—the new term for UFOs—following highly publicized cockpit videos by U.S. Navy pilots of strange aerial phenomena.[17] The report came as Netflix aired the docuseries *Top Secret UFO Projects: Declassified*. According to the *New York Times*,

> American intelligence officials have found no evidence that aerial phenomena witnessed by Navy pilots in recent years are alien spacecraft, but they still cannot explain the unusual movements that have mystified scientists and the military, according to senior administration officials briefed on the findings of a highly anticipated government report. The report determines that a vast majority of more than 120 incidents over the past two decades did not originate from any American military or other advanced U.S. government technology, the officials said.[18]

In an analysis of the report by Reasons to Believe, Mark Clark, professor emeritus of political science and director of the National Security Studies program at California State University, San Bernardino, writes that the report found no evidence that Russia or China was behind the UAPs, noting that Russia's military budget is a fraction of that of the United States, and China's military jet engines are fraught with problems. He goes on:

> The two most likely explanations remain if the previous pattern persists (more than 94 percent with natural explanations). First, these phenomena may have natural explanations. They may come from advanced research in either drone technology or electronic warfare. . . . This could be creating an environment where previously unobserved or rarely seen anomalies are quickly attributed to UFOs or ET instead of being examined in the context of drone technology. Or they could be a yet

unidentified natural phenomena, which Hugh Ross, Kenneth Samples and I detail in our book, *Lights in the Sky & Little Green Men.*

Second, the phenomena may be supernatural, as we document in our book. We have argued that the small number of residual UFO (RUFO) phenomena that cannot be explained otherwise may be demonic activity that appears to people who have opened doors to the occult.[19]

More on this later in this section.

Why is it so difficult to pin down hard evidence of UFO spacecraft or alien beings? Several well-known Bible scholars and Christian leaders believe, along with us, that these phenomena center around interdimensional or spiritual beings that can slip in and out of our dimension at will. Interdimensional hypothesis (IDH) is the name of this theory. The Bible is full of stories of angels, demons, spiritual beings and a host of otherworldly entities who intersect with our world—beings about which we know comparatively little.

Based on his examination of the subject, as detailed in his book *Lights in the Sky & Little Green Men: A Rational Christian Look at UFOs and Extraterrestrials,* co-author Hugh Ross agrees that most UFO reports can be explained by natural phenomena, military activity or hoaxes, but that a "residual" number involving millions of UFO and extraterrestrial sightings and encounters warrant further examination. He explains,

> When you look at the residual database, it's like what you see in the Navy pilot reports. These are objects that are moving at many times the speed of sound, sometimes as much as 18,000 to 20,000 miles per hour, yet they're observed to make sudden stops or sudden right-angle turns. No physical object can withstand that kind of acceleration. It would be shattered. Yet the Navy pilots don't observe that happening. Moreover, when observers see one of these UFOs going through the atmosphere

at such speeds, they never hear a sonic boom. They don't see any heat friction.[20]

When one of NASA's space shuttles reenters earth's atmosphere, Ross points out, a bright streak of light is visible, just as when a meteor cuts through the atmosphere. Not so with UFOs, he says. No bright streak. But there is still physical evidence:

> There are roughly two thousand documented cases where witnesses have seen these residual UFOs crashing into the earth. At the crash site, they see a crater, sometimes as much as a foot deep. Snow is melted and vegetation damaged. But as they look at the crater site, there is no debris, no artifact, from the crash of the UFO. All this is evidence that we're dealing with something real. Only something real would make a crater, melt snow, and damage vegetation.
>
> But it must be something nonphysical. If it was physical, there would be sonic booms, heat friction and debris at the crash site. So I conclude we're dealing with nonphysical reality. This also explains how they can make sharp angle turns at high velocity. If they're real but not physical, such motion is within the realm of possibility. So that's what we documented in this book.
>
> And I'm by no means alone. I can name six physicists who have devoted at least a decade to researching these phenomena, and they agree that we're dealing with something interdimensional, something from beyond the dimensions of the universe.[21]

How common is the belief in UFOs and extraterrestrials? SkyWatch TV host Derek P. Gilbert and his co-author, biblical researcher Josh Peck, point out that more Americans today "believe in ETs than in God."[22] In their book *The Day the Earth Stands Still: Unmasking the Old Gods Behind ETs, UFOs & the Official Disclosure Movement*, they cite research from the Barna Group:

About 9 percent of Americans have a biblical worldview, which is defined as holding six basic tenets of Christianity, like Christ lived a sinless life, was born of a virgin, literally rose from the dead, and so on—things that should be Christianity 101.

Yet according to a study done by the National Geographic Channel when they launched a new program on UFOs, they found that 36 percent of American adults believe that UFOs exist, and 77 percent believe we're being visited by extraterrestrials. So, four to eight times more American adults believe in ET than in God as He's revealed Himself in Scripture.

That is a problem! The enemy, the fallen realm, doesn't care what we believe so long as it's not the one thing that's true, which is that there's only one way to heaven and only one way to the Father—that is, through Jesus Christ.[23]

Fallen Angels and the Nephilim

Who are these interdimensional or spiritual beings? Here is one possibility:

> When human beings began to increase in number on the earth and daughters were born to them, the sons of God saw that the daughters of humans were beautiful, and they married any of them they chose. . . . The Nephilim were on the earth in those days—and also afterward—when the sons of God went to the daughters of humans and had children by them. They were the heroes of old, men of renown.
>
> Genesis 6:1–2, 4

Who were "the sons of God" who had children with "the daughters of humans"?

The late Dr. I. D. E. Thomas, pastor of several churches in Wales and Southern California and former BBC News correspondent, suggested that these "sons of God" were extraterrestrial entities, and that the Genesis passage refers to the "bizarre union between extraterrestrials and the women of earth."[24]

In his book *The Omega Conspiracy: Satan's Last Assault on God's Kingdom*, Thomas saw the Nephilim as "the superhuman offspring of the union,"[25] who appeared just before Noah's flood, and whose corruption was the main reason for God's judgment of the earth.

Centuries later the Nephilim emerged again—fewer this time—in the land of Canaan (see Numbers 13:32–33). Once again they were destroyed, this time by the children of Israel taking over the Promised Land. Thomas writes,

> The reappearance of their progeny would indicate that they returned to again contaminate the human race with their offspring. Evidence indicates that some of these Nephilim survived the second extermination. If so, where are they today? And are their extraterrestrial parents the aliens responsible for the UFOs? If the procreators of the Nephilim are to reinfest our world successfully, they must prepare mankind for the assault, for they face a more sophisticated human race.
>
> What greater ploy than to convince us that they are brothers of man travelling from distant worlds to invite us into the great galactic society? What greater stratagem than to awaken our imagination to the possibility of a supernatural union between aliens and the "daughters of man"?[26]

Correlation with the Occult

The phenomena of UFOs and extraterrestrials will only continue to increase to divert people's attention away from Jesus Christ and onto counterfeit pseudo-religious experiences and into occult entrapment.

Hugh Ross sees a connection between reporting sightings or encounters with extraterrestrials/UFOs and involvement in the occult or demonology:

> . . . whatever is behind witchcraft and the occult is also behind these "residual" UFO reports. We document this in our book,

making the point that the only people who have close encounters with "residual" UFOs are people involved in the occult, or have a close relative involved in the occult. Basically we say that our hypothesis about UFOs is scientifically testable. Get the occult out of your life and that'll be the end of your close UFO encounters. Bring the occult into your life and sooner or later you're likely to have these experiences.

So the fact that we see a correlation between the degree of occult activity and the percentage of the population that's having these kinds of encounters implies, indeed, that fallen angels are behind the occult. Demonology and witchcraft are responsible for this, and as we document in our book, when a person has close encounters, it's never beneficial; it's always deleterious. At best the encounters lead to recurring, terrifying nightmares. Worst case, people have been killed or injured in these encounters.[27]

Ross adds that some people who have encountered UFO beings have been put into trances and written "messages" to humanity from the UFO beings.

We have talked in various places about the "powerful delusion" the apostle Paul talks about in 2 Thessalonians 2:11—clearly an end-times reference. Jimmy Evans, former senior pastor at Trinity Fellowship Church in Amarillo, Texas, says he believes that the "powerful delusion" may actually refer to UFO deception:

Today we know through very reputable sources that there are UFOs. I mean, there's no doubt about it. Now the question is: Are they demons? I believe they're demonic. I do not believe they're extraterrestrials. But imagine this: Imagine the Rapture happens, and at the same time, UFOs appear in the sky. Not UFOs that dodge around, but they just park up in the sky all over the world. Which would get more attention?[28]

Evans, bestselling author of seventeen books, notes that there is a research group established by the Vatican Observatory at the Steward Observatory of the University of Arizona in Tucson. A consortium of institutions shares an instrument attached to a telescope, originally called the Large Binocular Telescope Near-Infrared Spectroscopic Utility with Camera and Integral Field Unit for Extragalactic Research—or LUCIFER for short. Although it was not owned by the Vatican, a firestorm of controversy caused it to be renamed LUCI in 2012.[29] Even so, Pastor Evans says,

> The Vatican is watching something that's coming. And they say, "When it arrives, they will be saving us and baptizing us and helping us understand God." I've heard people who believe this delusion and the lie that aliens actually put us here on earth, that they are our god, and that they're going to come back and say to the humans after the Rapture, "Those people were taken out of here because the world cannot continue to evolve with them because they're backward. They're out of date; they won't change. But we're here because we put you here, and here we are."
>
> The Bible says the false prophet calls down fire from heaven, and the image of the Antichrist moves and lives in front of people. There are all kinds of supernatural things happening in the end times.
>
> Today there are more people who believe in aliens than believe in God. And through all the movies of the last two decades, the world is set up for the UFO encounters to come. I really believe that the delusion could possibly be that UFOs put us here, that they're here to help us evolve, and that the Rapture was taking away people who wouldn't change.[30]

We cannot ignore a growing body of evidence suggesting that some UFOs sightings and extraterrestrial encounters are real. But instead of aliens visiting us from other planets, we have seen that these phenomena likely involve interdimensional beings, or what is known in Scripture as demonic or occult activity.

The Bible clearly warns that in the last days there will be many who will be led astray by "signs, and lying wonders" (2 Thessalonians 2:9 NKJV).

Don't be one of them.

TACTICS, TECHNIQUES AND PROCEDURES

1. **Plan regular family times** to discuss these issues. This will help prepare your children for what they will encounter at a secular institution of higher learning.

2. **Listen and critique.** When you hear or see something in the media regarding new technologies, evolution or UFOs, make sure to discover and reflect on what the Bible says about it.

3. **Have a contingency plan.** Plan now for what you and your family will need and do if your area is hit with an electromagnetic pulse (EMP) weapon.

PART 3

PERSONAL DECEPTION

11

The Hollywood Deception

"Pay no attention to that man behind the curtain!"

NOEL LANGLEY, screenwriter,
The Wizard of Oz

CAMP ARIFJAN
KUWAIT, SOMEWHERE IN THE TRAINING AREA
0600

We are running in formation performing morning PT, and a sergeant is calling out the cadence: "Standing tall and looking good, ought to march in Hollywood."

It brings my mind back to home and all the things that make home worth going back to.

The military is no different from the rest of the population in that we love entertainment, especially Hollywood movies. Hollywood over the years has put out some brilliant entertainment, but lately things have gone seriously awry, highlighted by the fact that wokeness, gender identity and Marxism have dominated the big screen in recent years.

I discovered the power of movies one time at a contemporary chapel service at Fort Campbell, Kentucky, where I was showing a clip of the 1970 war movie *Kelly's Heroes* starring Clint Eastwood and Donald Sutherland. The video clip was of a barrage of artillery firing at German units. I was showing it to emphasize a point in my sermon. Suddenly most of the 101st Airborne Division soldiers watching the clip dove to the floor to protect themselves from the incoming rounds. It was that real.

I was angry at myself for neglecting to understand that it was not smart to show such a clip to soldiers just coming back from actual combat.

Make no mistake about it. Movie images are powerful. And Hollywood—by which we mean the center of the film industry, but also include video on demand, streaming and subscription services—exerts a great deal of influence by producing material that promotes political and economic philosophies and greatly influences culture, education, religion and virtually every sphere of society.

In an iconic scene in *The Wizard of Oz*, Dorothy's dog, Toto,

sniffs out a side chamber and tugs open a curtain that reveals a diminutive old man behind a curtain who's talking into a microphone while pulling levers and pressing buttons. Once exposed, the man jumps up and yells into the microphone, "Pay no attention to that man behind the curtain!"[1]

That image of "that man behind the curtain"—the humbug pretending to be the mighty wizard of Oz—sums up nicely the deception coming out of studios and production companies today.

Movies as Conditioning

People watch the big screen (or smaller screens on their mobile devices) and *ooh!* and *ah!* over superheroes defending the planet, marvel at the inventive technology of CGI and are over-whelmed with the sheer genius of imagination and artistry. All this distracts from the reality here on planet earth—which is why we enjoy media entertainment.

All the while, "that man behind the curtain" is pulling levers to change our minds about what we believe and to prepare us for what is about to take place in the world. Whether we know it or not, movies are conditioning us for future events.

What Is Yet to Come

Take, for example, the plethora of end-of-the-world, one-world government; postapocalyptic war; alien invasion; intergalactic war; zombie invasion and similar films. Their sheer number is apparent just considering the number of trailers in a local theater for upcoming releases. Filmmakers and film buffs alike are immersed in that ultra-real world of supposed make-believe.

In the 2013 movie *The Book of Eli*, Denzel Washington's character, Eli, is told by a voice to carry the Bible to the West Coast thirty years after a nuclear holocaust. Along the dangerous path he must walk, he encounters many evil and bizarre characters trying to kill him for the Book, since in this time a Bible is rare and valuable. The plot is about a world that has undergone devastation and upheaval where there is no law or government.

Many other films depict dystopian nightmares in which good people struggle to stay alive. Are these make-believe, or are they, as the Bible tells us, about realities yet to come?

In the book of Revelation many things play out in a future that seems unbelievable. Some of these things include the rise of the Antichrist, global plagues, mega earthquakes, miraculous signs and wonders, demonic armies, meteorites hitting the earth, seas turning to blood, stars falling from the sky, the sun turning dark, the moon turning to blood and more earth-shattering phenomena of unprecedented magnitude.

Anti-Biblical Themes

Hollywood is not only preparing us for the future, but carefully orchestrating antibiblical and anti-Christian practices in its movies and television shows. Subtle deception is invading not only adult entertainment, but children's and young adult movies, too.

In the ending of the 2019 film *Star Wars: Episode IX—The Rise of Skywalker*, "the Star Wars franchise's first same-sex kiss lasts for only a few seconds as two minor female characters embrace within a celebratory crowd near the end."[2]

In 2021 Superman, the superhero who debuted in 1938, came out as bisexual.[3]

Like the proverbial frog in the kettle of water being heated gradually, we are at risk of being scalded to death.

It used to be back in the 1950s and '60s—for example, on *The Dick Van Dyke Show*—that a husband and wife could not even share the same bed on television. Now almost anything and everything goes. Even Christians are being lulled to sleep; and many, like frogs in the water, do not realize the danger.

We are addicted to television and movies. A study in England found that the average person views television a total of 78,000 hours over his or her lifetime.[4] Hollywood entertainment is one of the great distractions in life. It is the drug of choice to distract people from the stresses and strains of the real world. More on visual entertainment as the "media drug" shortly.

Powerful Influencers

What most people do not understand is that the powers of darkness appreciate this medium too, especially through the powerful influence of the deep state—defined by the Merriam-Webster Dictionary as "an alleged secret network of especially nonelected government officials and sometimes private entities (as in the financial services and defense industries) operating extralegally to influence and enact government policy" ⁵—the Central Intelligence Agency (CIA) and London-based Tavistock Institute of Human Relations.

In an article in the *Atlantic*, Nicholas Schou writes that one of the CIA's "foremost assets" is Hollywood:

> The agency has established a very active spin machine in the heart of the entertainment capital, which works strenuously to make sure the cloak-and-dagger world is presented in heroic terms. Since the mid-1990s, but especially after 9/11, American screenwriters, directors, and producers have traded positive portrayal of the spy profession in film or television projects for special access and favors at CIA headquarters.⁶

Daniel Estulin, an investigative journalist and the bestselling author of *The True Story of the Bilderberg Group*, writes that the Tavistock Institute, created in 1947 as the "psychological warfare arm of the British Royal Family," is the "world's center for mass brainwashing and social engineering activities."⁷

Employing psychological warfare and brainwashing techniques, the Tavistock Institute works with the CIA, the Frankfurt School and many government agencies, nongovernmental organizations, universities, think tanks, foundations, corporations and the pharmaceutical industry to "shape the destiny of the entire planet," Estulin writes, "and in the process, change the paradigm of modern society."⁸

Over the decades, the Tavistock Institute and its global network have worked to undermine America, Christianity and Western culture by helping engineer the 1960s anti-war movement, the "CIA's psychedelic revolution" and "drug-rock counterculture," the environmental movement and the ensuing moral freefall in society. Today, says Estulin, it is using Hollywood and the mass media to promote New Age beliefs in the occult, UFOs and extraterrestrials.[9]

The plan is known as the "Aquarian Conspiracy"—the title of a 1980 bestselling book, *The Aquarian Conspiracy*, which became a manifesto of the counterculture. And the goal, Estulin writes, is the "planned disintegration of the world economy by the most powerful people in the world," followed by the creation of a world government and a new global religion.[10] Controlling Hollywood and the mass media is key to the long-term objectives of the elite. He writes,

> The new religious forms will be a form of mystical anarchism, a religious experience much likened to satanic practice of the Nazis or the views of [Swiss psychologist and psychiatrist] Carl Jung. This is the "New Age," the "Age of Aquarius" preached by Tavistock and Frankfurt School with its eastern, mystical religious cults that had young, brainwashed converts flocking to embrace this degeneracy. Again, it is the television that provides the "social glue" that binds the minds of the population to their new religious forms.[11]

The Age of Aquarius he mentions is also the subject of the 1969 hit song by the 5th Dimension, "Aquarius (Let the Sunshine In)," drawn from the 1967 musical *Hair*, speaking of Jupiter aligning with Mars. Astrologers do not agree on when the Age of Aquarius started, or even whether it has started. But interestingly, on December 21, 2020, several decades after that hit song, an alignment occurred in the heavens hailed by the media as the new "Christmas star." Some said that this conjunction of Jupiter and Saturn heralded the dawning of the Age of Aquarius.

One astrologer, according to bestselling prophecy author Thomas Horn, opined that the planetary conjunction in 2020 has a major role to play in this decade, "and the outcome of this decade will create a new order which will be applied for the next seventy years from 2030 to the end of this century."[12]

SkyWatch TV host Sharon K. Gilbert reminds us of the implications:

> Dr. Klaus Schwab [founder of the World Economic Forum] believes that our world is about to enter a New Age; a great New World Order, that precipitates from something he calls the Great Reset. . . . Let's put all these clues together. Jupiter's conjunction with Saturn on December 21, 2020—the winter solstice—somehow announced the arrival of a New Age. . . . The governments will look to an overarching body like the World Economic Forum to lead them into this new order, right?[13]

Alex Newman, the award-winning international journalist and author, sees Hollywood programming as "just that: programming":

> They are programming you to respond in a particular way to a particular thing. They are programming you to think about a particular issue in a particular way. And this is nothing new; it's simply become more advanced over the years. If you look at the bigwigs in Hollywood, what you will find is they are very well connected to the deep state.[14]

Jimmy Evans points out that Hollywood films like *The Da Vinci Code* (2006) persuaded many people that Jesus did not die on the cross but survived, married Mary Magdalene and had children. Other programming explores the ideas of UFOs and extraterrestrials populating the universe:

> *Star Trek* is an example. The movies and TV shows tend to make us think there are going to be thousands and thousands of years of human history, that we're going to evolve, that we're going to go into the universe and take over, that evolution is true. But

that's not what the Bible says. The Bible says there is going to be an "end of the age." That's what the disciples were asking Jesus in the Olivet Discourse: "When is the end going to be?" And that is when Jesus went into very specific signs.

I think Hollywood has been part of the Antichrist system of convincing humankind that we'll evolve on our own. This is what humanism says: "We don't need God. Man will save himself. Man is the measure of all things." That's the mantra of humanism. And Hollywood has done a masterful job of pounding that message into people so that many have lost their faith in God.[15]

Guarding against the "Media Drug"

The Bible is explicit about how we are to approach secular entertainment. In Mark 13:32–37 (NKJV), the Lord talks about His return to earth and our own disposition:

> "Of that day and hour no one knows, not even the angels in heaven, nor the Son, but only the Father. Take heed, watch and pray; for you do not know when the time is. It is like a man going to a far country, who left his house and gave authority to his servants, and to each his work, and commanded the door-keeper to watch. Watch therefore, for you do not know when the master of the house is coming—in the evening, at midnight, at the crowing of the rooster, or in the morning—lest, coming suddenly, he find you sleeping. And what I say to you, I say to all: Watch!"

One of the real dangers of multimedia entertainment, including videos, videogames, television shows, reality TV and movies, is the lulling to sleep of our senses until something catastrophic takes place—and then it is too late.

This, as we call it, is the "media drug." On one end of the spectrum, it deadens our senses to reality and keeps us focused on things that, for the most part, are unimportant. On the other end of the spectrum, this drug influences people in the direction that the powers behind the scenes want them to take. Yes, it is a propaganda tool.

Jesus said,

> "The eye is the lamp of the body. If your eyes are healthy, your whole body will be full of light. But if your eyes are unhealthy, your whole body will be full of darkness. If then the light within you is darkness, how great is that darkness!"
>
> Matthew 6:22–23

What we watch has tremendous influence over our lives. The seeds planted as we consume media and entertainment will take root and grow for good or bad, depending on what we are seeing.

Proverbs 4:23 tells us to "keep your heart with all diligence, for out of it spring the issues of life" (NKJV). The eye is the window to your soul and heart—not your physical heart, but your spiritual heart, that central part of your inner being that relates to God and generates emotions and desires. It is also the place where evil is produced, according to Jesus:

> "It is from within, out of a person's heart, that evil thoughts come—sexual immorality, theft, murder, adultery, greed, malice, deceit, lewdness, envy, slander, arrogance and folly. All these evils come from inside and defile a person."
>
> Mark 7:21–23

The vital thing to remember, then, is always to "guard your heart" (Proverbs 4:23). Be very careful what you watch, for those very things go through your eyes and into your soul. Remember that "the eye is the lamp of the body" (Matthew 6:22) and the gateway into the soul.

Make a pledge right now to watch only those things that are healthy and vital to your soul.

Epicenter of Influence

There are many layers of deception, as we have seen, when it comes to entertainment and the media.

The media is so powerful that many government agencies, both foreign and domestic, as well as subversive groups around the globe, are determined to weaponize it for their own hidden agendas. This weapon is pointed at unknowing populations to condition them for the coming world government.

David Heavener, who has directed, produced and starred in more than fifty movies and is the founder of David Heavener Ministries, calls Hollywood "an empty shell." He explains,

> You've got the political system, you've got the financial system, you have the religious system and the cultural system. There are more systems, but those are the four main ones. I called it the satanic pyramid. Powerful forces use these systems and Hollywood as a vehicle to brainwash society. It's mind control.[16]

It is no secret that the Pentagon established the Entertainment Liaison Office in 1948 and the CIA followed up with a comparable position in 1996.

Matthew Alford points out in an article for the British *Independent* that Hollywood and the U.S. government have long been cozy:

> Washington DC has long been a source of intriguing plots for filmmakers and LA has been a generous provider of glamour and glitz to the political class. . . . Files we obtained, mainly through the U.S. Freedom of Information Act, show that between 1911 and 2017, more than 800 feature films received

support from the U.S. Government's Department of Defense (DoD), a significantly higher figure than previous estimates indicate. These included blockbuster franchises such as *Transformers*, *Iron Man*, and *The Terminator*.[17]

I will never forget the morning in the spring of 2001when I was sitting in my brigade staff meeting at Fort Benning, Georgia. My unit at the time was the Basic Combat Training Brigade, responsible to conduct basic training on Sand Hill at Fort Benning. As I listened to the briefing, something caught my attention. Apparently, the cast members of an upcoming film were going through "basic training" in preparation, and it was happening right there at Fort Benning.

The film was *We Were Soldiers*, starring Mel Gibson and Sam Elliott, one of many movies using military hardware and support.

It did not take me long to make my way to the training site. Sure enough, the first person I saw was Mel Gibson on the firing line, along with Sam Elliott and other actors.

I pointed out to Gibson that, even though as a marksman he never missed in the movies, he was not hitting the targets very well in training. He laughed and replied, "Yeah, I hit everything in the movies."

Elliott chided him and said that he was outshooting Mel. And when Sam was done shooting, he came up to me, looked me in the eye, shook my hand firmly and said in his deep, resonant voice, "Pleased to meet you, sir!"

Later I discovered that not only the command at Fort Benning but the powers in the Pentagon were supporting the making of *We Were Soldiers*, providing use of Fort Benning facilities and personnel.

The movie turned out to be a great recruiting tool for the U.S. Army for years to come, just as *Top Gun* with Tom Cruise was an effective recruiting tool for the U.S. Navy.

The power, emotion and raw energy of movies like this can persuade, inform and shape people's lives. Their influence does not have to be negative. But there is a dark side, a deep undercurrent in Hollywood that uses the power of movies to shape the culture for its own purposes—political and otherwise.

Hollywood, the CIA and the mainstream media work together as an unholy alliance in sending out propaganda and covert messages. Read the following passage from the *Atlantic* regarding the collaboration between Hollywood and Langley, Virginia (the location of CIA headquarters):

> As Hollywood became increasingly embedded with Langley following 9/11, CIA employees often saw their public-affairs colleagues giving various celebrities personalized tours of the headquarters. "I can't tell you how many times this happened," recalled the former CIA officer John Kiriakou. He would regularly bump into a parade of Hollywood types, including Harrison Ford and Ben Affleck. He often wondered why these actors were allowed to walk around a top-secret facility. "Because he's going to be playing a CIA guy in a movie? That's the criteria now? You just have to be a friend of the agency and you can come in and walk around?" In the meantime, people who are undercover are having to walk through the halls with their hands over their faces because these people aren't cleared. It's insane.[18]

Some would explain that this relationship helps viewers see the CIA in a more favorable light, but there are more sinister issues afoot.

Both the Department of Defense and the CIA use films to promote certain attitudes and worldviews they think are important.

Wielding the Sword of the Spirit

Given the many layers of deception involving mainstream media entertainment, it is critical to wield the sword of the Spirit, pray in the Spirit and walk in authority over the enemy to ensure that you and your family are not deceived in this age of confusion.

Consider, for example, the blockbuster movie *E.T. the Extra-Terrestrial*, a science fiction film produced and directed by Steven Spielberg. It tells the story of Elliott, a boy who befriends an extraterrestrial, E.T., who is stranded on earth. Shortly after its release in 1982, the movie surpassed *Star Wars* to become the highest-grossing film of all time—a record it held for eleven years until *Jurassic Park* surpassed it in 1993. *E.T.* is regarded as one of the greatest films of all time, nominated for nine Oscars, including Best Picture. It is sweet and touching.

Yet *E.T.*, says film director and actor David Heavener, is an early example of how countless Hollywood movies over the decades have prepared the world for extraterrestrial "disclosure." He explains,

> If you think about it, back when the film came out, there was this cute little alien that everyone embraced, brought into their homes and loved him, but that was the Antichrist's way of connecting them to an alien being, which is actually demonic. So when UFO disclosure happens and the Antichrist, who is going to be a hybrid, promises us all that we'll live 500 years and we'll have super intelligence and whatever, people will go for it.[19]

For people to fall for the lies of the Antichrist, they will already have a distorted point of view regarding God. Heavener goes on to say,

> This is a manifestation of the "powerful delusion" described in 2 Thessalonians 2:11. From my reading of Scripture, the delusion is that your connection, your viewpoint, your idea of God is diluted. That's the great delusion, because without that, you're never going to fall for the illusion created by demonic forces. The illusion really is, when the Antichrist comes in, he's going to say, "I'm going to save you. I'm God. And I'm going to help you."

That's really an illusion, right? The delusion is that we have succumbed. We have given in to the Antichrist system, saying, "Jesus is illegal. It's more important to abide by man's laws because it will help me and be better for me than abiding by God's laws."[20]

TACTICS, TECHNIQUES AND PROCEDURES

The question remains, What are we to do and how are we to fight the addiction and "media drug" that not only deadens our senses to reality, but makes us vulnerable to the propaganda being fed us by the powers behind the scenes?

1. **Inventory what movies you watch.** Ensure that you and your family are watching only entertainment that is wholesome, educational and uplifting. Research the movie or program before watching on honest websites like movieguide.org or pluggedin.com that evaluate it through the filter of a biblical worldview.

2. **Find other activities besides television and movies.** Get involved in activities like sports, games, outdoor activities like hiking or fishing, or any number of hobbies.

3. **Read and discuss the Bible.** Gather the family each night not only to read the Bible, but to apply it and discuss how it affects everyone's lives.

4. **Find and watch Christian-produced movies and programs.** The genre has greatly improved and there are good ones out there these days. *The Chosen*, for example, is an excellent multiseason television drama based on the life of Jesus and has great messages.

12

The Elijah Principle

One of the great uses of Twitter and Facebook will be to prove
at the Last Day that prayerlessness was not from lack of time.

JOHN PIPER, theologian, pastor, chancellor,
Bethlehem College & Seminary

WINTER EARLY 1990S
1–37 ARMOR BATTALION HEADQUARTERS
VILSECK, GERMANY

I do not know if it is just me or if the burnout I am feeling is
hitting the rest of the M1A1 Abrams tank unit to which I am
assigned.

The pace has been at breakneck speed without a pause for
months. We trained up at the Grafenwoehr Training Area in
preparation for the ultimate test at the CMTC in Hohenfels,
Bavaria, under the 7th Army Training Command. Now we have
just returned from long weeks of nonstop heavy training with
outstanding results. We have achieved great victories over the
opposing forces, something that is rarely done.

165

We are in some downtime to refit, perform maintenance and maybe take some leave in preparation for the next cycle of events. I am in my office in the morning, looking over my calendar, getting ready for counseling with my soldiers and getting some office work done. I decide to walk down the hall and check in with everyone when I notice one of our majors in his office, legs stretched out, feet up on the desk, staring out the window at the cold, dreary winter day.

He is our S-3 operations officer, a job that is very demanding and requires long hours. I chat with him to see if everything is all right, and notice the same symptoms I am experiencing: weariness, bags under the eyes from lack of sleep, and the general malaise that hits you after slowing down after a great victory. He indicates that he is okay, but I know better.

I go about my business, and about three hours later I look into that same office and see the major in the same position, staring out the window. I chuckle to myself, knowing he just needs to be left alone with his thoughts and let his mind and body rest.

We all need some rest and a break, even for a short time.

I am learning that what affects your body (tiredness) also affects the state of your mind and soul and spirit. The higher intensity of stress, the more your whole being reacts to it. The mind, body and soul are all interconnected and intertwined:

> Now may the God of peace Himself sanctify you completely; and may your whole spirit, soul, and body be preserved blameless at the coming of our Lord Jesus Christ.
>
> 1 Thessalonians 5:23 NKJV

Medical professionals tell us that many people in the hospital are there due to stress. In fact, chronic stress is linked to six leading causes of death, according to the American Psychological

Association: heart disease, cancer, lung ailments, accidents, cirrhosis of the liver and suicide.[1]

We deceive ourselves into thinking we can keep piling more and more work and stressors on ourselves and not pay the consequences. We wonder why our bodies begin to break down under the load.

This is just one form of personal self-deception. There are many others.

Overcoming Personal Deception

The mind that God gave us is a powerful tool for good and evil. We must continually present our minds to God for renewal and edification, as Paul exhorts us:

> Do not conform to the pattern of this world, but be transformed by the renewing of your mind. Then you will be able to test and approve what God's will is—his good, pleasing and perfect will.
>
> Romans 12:2

With the breakdown of morals in society, the breakup of the family, the pandemic, earthquakes, fires, floods, economic upheaval and the stresses of daily life, our minds along with our souls and bodies are reeling from the overwhelming onslaught of uncertainty.

Chaos, confusion and fear now reign supreme on the earth. People do not know which way to turn or whom to believe. For many, the truth has become relative to what you believe and who you are. Even in Christian circles, the Bible has become more and more irrelevant.

Could it be that, in our postmodern scientific age, we have lost our way to God? Amid the chaos, confusion and fear, we doubt that there is a God, and even if we do believe in Him, do we trust Him and His Word? And if we trust His Word, do we follow it and, more importantly, follow Him? Many of us are like Pontius Pilate, under terrible pressure from the crowd, when he asked Jesus, "What is truth?" and then walked away, not waiting for the answer (John 18:38).

According to Gallup, only 24 percent of Christians in America believe the Bible is the "literal" Word of God. A total of 47 percent of Christians in America believe it is the "inspired" Word of God, but that not all of it should be taken literally.[2]

The reason deception is prevalent in our world today is that we have lost our trust in God's Word. With that loss of trust comes a loss of faith, since "faith comes by hearing, and hearing by the word of God" (Romans 10:17 NKJV).

The Great Apostasy

Dr. Robert Jeffress believes we are seeing what the apostle Paul describes as "the falling away" (2 Thessalonians 2:3 NKJV) of professing Christians. He says:

> I've seen an interesting thing happen just over the last ten years about gay marriage. It used to be, when you talked to Christians who embraced a redefinition of marriage, and you pointed out Bible verses to them that talk specifically about the issue, they would try to offer another interpretation of those passages. But now you offer a biblical definition of marriage and say, "This is what the Bible says," and they don't try to refute the Bible. They say, "The Bible is absolutely wrong on this."
>
> That, to me, is a huge digression—going from agreeing that the Bible is the Word of God, but having a different interpretation, to saying, "I don't care what the Bible says." There's a hardness of heart taking place among God's own people.[3]

A member of Jeffress's church for more than five decades, the world-renowned evangelist Billy Graham, one of the most recognized religious figures of the twentieth century, once estimated that even in evangelical churches, only about half the congregation is "truly born again," says Jeffress. He adds:

> I wouldn't be surprised if that's true. The fact is, Jesus predicted that the road to heaven is very narrow, and that few will enter the narrow gate by which we must be saved. Jesus predicted that many on Judgment Day will say, "Lord, Lord, we did this" and "we did that," and He will say, "Depart from Me. I never knew you." I think there's going to be a horrific surprise awaiting many people who think they're saved, who in fact aren't saved.[4]

Paul says that in the last days, believers will be deceived because "they refused to love the truth" (2 Thessalonians 2:10).

There are many puzzling things going on with society in these last times—for instance, in the Roman Catholic Church, one of the most conservative institutions on the planet. The Reverend William Saunders writes for the Catholic News Agency,

> The Church teaches, "Human life is sacred because from its beginning it involves the creative action of God and it remains forever in a special relationship with the Creator, who is its sole end. God alone is the Lord of life from its beginning until its end: no one can under any circumstance claim for himself the right directly to destroy an innocent human being" ("Donum vitae," 5).[5]

How, then, can the Roman Catholic leadership allow adherents and even political leaders who support abortion to continue their membership while espousing a doctrine diametrically opposed to their beliefs?

Loving truth is key in not being deceived in the end times. If we are focused on knowing and loving Jesus and the truth that surrounds the Gospel, we will never be deceived. In the book of Revelation, the apostle John clearly lays out the formula:

> Then I heard a loud voice in heaven say:
> "Now have come the salvation and the power and the kingdom of our God, and the authority of his Messiah. For the accuser of our brothers and sisters, who accuses them before our God day and night, has been hurled down. They triumphed over him by the blood of the Lamb and by the word of their testimony; they did not love their lives so much as to shrink from death. Therefore rejoice, you heavens and you who dwell in them! But woe to the earth and the sea, because the devil has gone down to you! He is filled with fury, because he knows that his time is short."
>
> Revelation 12:10–12

We conquer Satan and deception "by the blood of the Lamb and by the word of [our] testimony" (verse 11). This means that in the war against these dark powers, we must ask the Lord to cover us by the blood He shed on the cross for our sins, and that we may have to testify about the love of Christ for this world to those who may execute us for that testimony.

The question of life and death may come down to either acknowledging Christ as our Lord or facing execution at the hands of the followers of the Antichrist.

Spiritual Checkup

I experienced another episode of truth, tiredness and training back in the early 1990s, when I was stationed at 1–37 Armor Battalion Headquarters in Germany. Our unit deployed to the CMTC for a thirty-day nonstop training exercise. My assistant and I had been going for three weeks almost nonstop and were exhausted, strained and touchy.

When you come to that point in your life, it is as if spirituality has flown the coop. What I needed at that time (and did not know it) was rest and renewal. It was like coming home from war.

At that time an Observer Controller (OC) flagged me as a casualty for not being at a designated place at a certain time. I became unglued and actually lunged at the OC. I had to be restrained, put on a gurney and transported to the rear. I was literally fit to be tied!

There was no excuse for my behavior. But I was dirty, muddy and beyond tired. My spirit and soul felt the same. At that point I did not care about truth—or anything else, for that matter.

There are times in our life when, if we are not careful and observant, we can be deceived into thinking we are okay, but we are not. We may, as I was, be exhausted and fit to be tied. That is when it is time for a spiritual checkup and a faith inventory.

If you are wondering what happened to me in Germany after I lost it, I recovered completely after a hot shower, food and sleep. It is amazing how rest and recuperation can refresh you—body, mind and soul. Whatever affects one part of us affects the rest.

We all need to be watchful and prayerful that we do not get to that point and fall into deception. With the world in upheaval and turmoil, many are looking at events in fear and trepidation, wondering what to do.

Our focus needs to be centered on Christ and Christ alone. Remember when Jesus was walking on water and, in faith, Peter got out of the boat and walked on the lake toward Jesus. Then Peter lost focus and began to sink. Jesus reached out His hand and caught him, saying, "You of little faith, why did you doubt?" (Matthew 14:31).

Elijah Is Coming Back!

Elijah is the perfect example of a biblical figure who went through a very rough season of doubt in his life.

He had just won a great victory by confronting King Ahab, setting up a magnificent competition between God and Baal—"If the LORD is God, follow him; but if Baal is God, follow him" (1 Kings 18:21)—and showing the Lord as the one true God. Elijah then executed 450 prophets of Baal, winning Israel back to the Lord. But Queen Jezebel took exception to him and vowed to kill him the next day.

Elijah took off like a scared rabbit and ran far into the wilderness. He was tired, hungry, depressed and at the end of his rope.

> He came to a broom bush, sat down under it and prayed that he might die. "I have had enough, LORD," he said. "Take my life; I am no better than my ancestors." Then he lay down under the bush and fell asleep.
>
> All at once an angel touched him and said, "Get up and eat." He looked around, and there by his head was some bread baked over hot coals, and a jar of water. He ate and drank and then lay down again.
>
> The angel of the LORD came back a second time and touched him and said, "Get up and eat, for the journey is too much for you." So he got up and ate and drank. Strengthened by that food, he traveled forty days and forty nights until he reached Horeb, the mountain of God. There he went into a cave and spent the night.
>
> 1 Kings 19:4–9

Notice a few things in this passage about deception.

First, Elijah was not himself after a great victory; he was exhausted. When you are depleted in energy, as Jesus said, "The spirit is willing, but the flesh is weak" (Matthew 26:41).

Second, even though Elijah knew the power of God, he no longer cared, and seemed not to remember what God had done the day before.

Third, he wanted to die. We say this all the time in the U.S. Army: Don't make a permanent decision for a temporary problem.

What was God's solution? Water, food, rest and, most importantly, His own word. Elijah heard the word of the Lord in a still, small voice in what I call the cave of deliverance:

> The Lord said, "Go out and stand on the mountain in the presence of the Lord, for the Lord is about to pass by."
>
> Then a great and powerful wind tore the mountains apart and shattered the rocks before the Lord, but the Lord was not in the wind. After the wind there was an earthquake, but the Lord was not in the earthquake. After the earthquake came a fire, but the Lord was not in the fire. And after the fire came a gentle whisper. When Elijah heard it, he pulled his cloak over his face and went out and stood at the mouth of the cave. Then a voice said to him, "What are you doing here, Elijah?"
>
> 1 Kings 19:11–13

The Elijah principle is this: After every great victory and spiritual high, prepare for a battle and a spiritual low.

God asked Elijah the same question He is asking us: What are you doing here in your disbelief, despite My Word, power, love and might?

The greatest weapon formed against deception in these end times is total and unquestioning belief in the infallible Word of God, the Bible.

Mary Ann Peluso McGahan, television host and advisor to Battle Ready Ministries, says now is a time of "pruning, purging and purifying for the Body of Christ." She explains,

> We are in a crucible of testing, and the Spirit of the Lord is saying, "Get your house in order." He is blowing a trumpet to

the Body of Christ. He's going to deal with the world simultaneously, but there are two things going on right now. I have sensed that through your books [this one and *The Military Guide to Armageddon*], God is going to awaken people to a new commitment.

You can't get into the army or military and not be intentional. You've got to know what you're getting into. You've got to count the cost before you sign up for service. There's a calling for enlisting in the army of God, and we're being tested right now—not so God can see what we're made of, but so *we* can know what we're made of. We need to sit down and intentionally get our houses in order.[6]

McGahan says she is reminded of Isaiah 30:9–10:

"These are rebellious people, deceitful children, children unwilling to listen to the LORD's instruction. They say to the seers, 'See no more visions!' and to the prophets, 'Give us no more visions of what is right! Tell us pleasant things; prophesy illusions.'"

My concern today is that while the Word is going out and the trumpet is being blown and people are yelling, "Amen," and crying and screaming for revival, how many are living it in their everyday lives? How many are saying, "God, I want to be holy"? I believe that the letters on the Ark of the Covenant today would be R.I.H.—*Repentance, Intimacy* and *Holiness*. I believe that God is giving a last trumpet call because once this apostasy goes full bloom, we know what happens.

These people will go through the Tribulation, and many of them will be saved, but they will have a hard time. There will be a harvest during the first three and a half years of the Tribulation, but at that time it's too late to escape the persecution of the Antichrist. I hear the Spirit of God saying, "The apostasy has started, and it's time for each individual to grab hold of God in this hour and not be deceived." I believe we're at the front door of the great falling away.[7]

Jimmy Evans believes that the prophet Elijah will be one of the "two witnesses" described in Revelation 11:3–12 who will proclaim the Gospel for 1,260 days during the first half of the Tribulation.[8]

These verses say the two witnesses will have the power to stop rain from falling upon the earth, "to turn the waters into blood and to strike the earth with every kind of plague as often as they want" (verse 6). Further, against those who attempt to harm them, "fire comes from their mouths and devours their enemies" (verse 5). But the two witnesses will be killed, and their dead bodies will lie in the square for three and a half days, until they stand on their feet, striking "terror" into the onlookers (verse 11), and are called up to heaven (see verse 12).

Many prophecy teachers see the two witnesses as Moses and Elijah. Malachi 4:5 says Elijah will be sent by God to Israel "before the coming of the great and terrible day of the LORD" (NASB). Jimmy Evans agrees:

Elijah's coming back. He's going to be one of the two witnesses. What an example of godliness! Jesus said in Mark 8:38, "If you're ashamed of Me in this adulterous and sinful generation, I'll be ashamed of you when I return in the glory of My Father and His holy angels." Elijah is an example of a man who stood against Jezebel, who stood against all the ungodly forces of his age, and God honored him for it. He had a tremendous impact on that society.

I believe you're on the offense or you're on the defense. If you're on the offense, you're living to make a difference for God. If you're on the defense, you're hanging on to the end. There's more and more pressure—social media, the fear of man and much more—for people to compromise their faith. They're vicious, and we're under incredible pressure.

I would say to everyone reading this book, make up your mind. Commit your life to Christ. Live for God. Jesus said, "If anyone wants to follow Me, let him deny himself, take up his cross and follow Me" (Matthew 16:24). When Jesus said, "Take up your cross," He hadn't died on the cross yet. The cross is a death instrument to put to death the things that are keeping us from living for God. So it's a day to dedicate ourselves to living for God. Elijah is a perfect example.[9]

TACTICS, TECHNIQUES AND PROCEDURES

How do we dedicate ourselves to living for God as Elijah did? Perform a spiritual self-inventory.

And here are some things you can do right now:

1. **Look at your life in light of God's Word.** Do you believe the Bible is the Word of God? If not, why not? If so, are you following its principles, such as Jesus' command to take up your cross and follow Him (see Matthew 16:24)? Are you a follower of Christ? What does it mean to follow Him?

2. **Take an inventory of your schedule.** Is it sustainable over the long haul? Is what you are doing God's plan for your life? Is there time in your schedule for being alone with Him and hearing His instructions for your day? What time works best for you to spend this vital time with the Holy Spirit each day?

3. **Do you follow a daily reading plan of the Bible?** Is it working for you? Are you daily applying those things you are reading? Remember that "faith without works is dead" (James 2:26 NKJV). Memorize Scripture every day, even if it is the same one repeatedly, until you know it by heart. Start with John 3:16.

4. **If you are married and have children, have you piled so many things onto your schedule that you don't have time for one-on-one time with your spouse and kids?** Do you have a family night when there are no interruptions or phone calls? Are you ministering the Word of God daily to your family?

13

The Battlespace of the Mind

But I see another law at work in me, waging war against the law of my mind and making me a prisoner of the law of sin at work within me.

ROMANS 7:23

FALL 2005
C-130 TRANSPORT, SOMEWHERE OVER THE DESERT OF SOUTHERN IRAQ

I am accustomed to finding myself in dangerous and hazardous situations so I can accompany the troops into battle and beyond. On this occasion, I board a C-130 four-engine transport aircraft that many of our soldiers use to jump into battle. It is just me, my assistant and the flight crew flying over the desert of southern Iraq from Baghdad International Airport on our way to Camp Arifjan in Kuwait.

Suddenly the large aircraft nosedives straight down and lands in the middle of the desert in an unscheduled (to say the least!) stop. The crew chief asks my assistant and me to deplane and wait while they unload the crates from the back of the aircraft.

"What's going on?" I ask.

"Sir, we landed abruptly out here in the middle of nowhere when I discovered on my munitions checklist that we were carrying explosives that detonate at ten thousand feet."

I gulp hard. "Thanks, chief, for double-checking that list and taking care of us."

Traveling through combat zones and engaging with my soldiers in Saudi Arabia, Iraq, Afghanistan, Kuwait and Central America, I have gotten on transportation that moves through the battlespace on the ground, in the air and by sea. These transports and weapon systems include M1A1 tanks, Bradley Fighting Vehicles, armored personnel carriers, Blackhawk helicopters, twin engine jets and four-prop transport planes such as the C-130 Hercules, the C-5 Galaxy and the C-17 Globemaster.

Moving through the ongoing battlespaces of war helped me gain a perspective that few in the military could appreciate or experience. But I learned a valuable lesson that day in the desert of southern Iraq never to take anything for granted when flying or traveling through battlespace in combat, and always to remain vigilant, praying constantly.

In other words, watch and pray.

Multidimensional Battlespace

During many years in my military career, I gained an entirely new appreciation for the word *battlespace*. Here is the military's definition:

The commander's conceptual view of the area and factors, which he must understand to apply combat power, protect the force, and complete the mission. It encompasses all applicable aspects of air, sea, space, land, and information operations, as well as the human dimension, that the commander must consider in planning and executing military operations. The battlespace dimensions can change over time as the mission expands or contracts, according to operational objectives and force composition. Battlespace provides the commander a mental framework for analyzing and selecting courses of action for employing military forces in relationship to time, tempo, and depth.[1]

Combat today is fought in nonlinear fashion; the military names the place of modern war a "battlespace." What most people do not understand about the science and tactics of modern warfare is that it is no longer linear, meaning that your enemy may not be lined up in front of you on a battlefield as in the Civil War and other battles of long ago. In chapter 10 we noted that the reason so many died in World War I is that soldiers were using Napoleonic tactics from the previous wars in Europe (marching in rank and column), rushing in a frontal assault against new technical marvels like the machine gun and advanced artillery—which simply obliterated them.

The truth is, the military must fight in the air, on the land, over and under the water, and even in cyber and outer space to win today's battles and wars. There is no such thing as a frontline anymore because the battle is raging all around us, even in the invisible realm.

There is much biblical teaching regarding the battlefield of the mind and the spiritual warfare that takes place in the space between your ears.

What the military's definition (above) means to us believers is that spiritual warfare, by its very definition, is fought on multiple levels—in the mind as well as the body, soul and spirit. In other words, it is multidimensional. You must be empowered by the Spirit of God to fight the good fight of faith. You will never engage the enemy properly—not to mention win—with your natural reasoning or education, no matter how brilliant you are.

SkyWatch TV host and author Derek Gilbert says,

> The enemy is playing eleven-dimensional chess while we're playing checkers in two dimensions, so we are totally out of our depth if we try to fight them on our own terms.[2]

In this chapter we are exploring the battlespace of the mind. So let's ask this question: What is the biblical definition of *mind*? The International Standard Bible Encyclopedia Online tells us that "we look in vain in the Old Testament and New Testament for anything like scientific precision in the employment of terms which are meant to indicate mental operations."[3]

But believers in the West try to break down divisions scientifically between mind, spirit, soul and body. Ancient peoples of the Near East had no such idea; they saw the mind, body and soul as an integrated whole. So we must not try to transfer contemporary thinking about the mind, brain and intellect into the ancient Scriptures.

Some point to Hebrews 4:12 NKJV:

> The word of God is living and powerful, and sharper than any two-edged sword, piercing even to the division of soul and spirit, and of joints and marrow, and is a discerner of the thoughts and intents of the heart.

What did the writer mean by "the division of soul and spirit"? The best interpretation of this verse by many top scholars is that it is practically impossible to divide between an integrated whole—but with God and His Word, all things are possible. The following statement from BibleRef.com sums it up nicely:

The Word of God can even separate spiritual things which seem completely intertwined, such as the soul and spirit. This is not meant to be literal, as the Bible often uses these terms interchangeably. Rather, this is a graphic explanation of how completely God's Word can distinguish between the godly and ungodly. To man, the soul and spirit seem indistinguishable, but the Word of God can—metaphorically—even discern between these. This incredible "cutting" power of Scripture is therefore a tool to separate our very thoughts into good and evil.[4]

How is this important in reference to deception? In three ways.

1. Train Your Whole Self

First, we must understand that our minds are not just our brains, as in the phrase *He has lost his mind*. If the mind is our integrated, whole self, then we must train our whole self not to fall into deception or sin.

A war is raging in our inner members, or within ourselves, between that which is an enemy of God (our flesh) and that which is connected to God (our spirit). The apostle Paul refers to our flesh, or old self, as the "old man":

> Put off, concerning your former conduct, the old man which grows corrupt according to the deceitful lusts, and be renewed in the spirit of your mind, and that you put on the new man which was created according to God, in true righteousness and holiness.

Ephesians 4:22–24 NKJV

2. Recognize the Supernatural Dimension

Second, we must recognize that the war raging "against the law of my mind" (Romans 7:23) is the war in our battlespace that includes multiple dimensions, including the spiritual dimension, in which angels and demons reside.

In John 1:51 Jesus says, "Very truly I tell you, you will see 'heaven open, and the angels of God ascending and descending on' the Son of Man." Clearly, the supernatural realm or dimension is fully engaged and active all around us, while we remain unaware.

The story in 2 Kings 6 illustrates this fact. Elisha's servant was afraid of the army surrounding them and cried out to his master.

> And Elisha prayed, "Open his eyes, LORD, so that he may see."
> Then the LORD opened the servant's eyes, and he looked and saw the hills full of horses and chariots of fire all around Elisha.
>
> verse 17

3. Ask God to Open Your Eyes

Third, we need know that living in the midst of the supernatural is key to unlocking the door that leads to a powerful victory over deception. That door is unlocked when we move with great passion and energy toward God and away from the forces of evil. The secret is asking God, like Elisha, to open our eyes to what is really going on around us.

Paul Pickern, founder and CEO of All Pro Pastors International, has this spiritual counsel:

> To be victorious over deception, the best way to prepare is to know God's Word and to have a strong prayer life, a real communion with God in which you're walking with the Holy Spirit. You have the Word of God and you have a relationship with the Holy Spirit so you can recognize the enemy using discernment.
>
> The other important thing is associating with true believers, having relationships and actual accountability and encouragement from them, which is a form of training to build yourself up, and, of course, to stay on top of what is going on.

Be aware; study, read. Don't keep your head in the sand. Don't follow just one group or teaching. You need to know what the enemy is doing as well as what God is doing. Don't just sit back and do nothing. One of the most powerful things is to be a proactive disciple of Christ in sharpening others and making disciples.

Do all these things combined and you won't be deceived.[5]

How Big Is Our God?

An event even more powerful than the account of Elisha seeing the horses and chariots of fire surrounding him happened to Joshua as he pursued his enemies:

> On the day the LORD gave the Amorites over to Israel, Joshua said to the LORD in the presence of Israel: "Sun, stand still over Gibeon, and you, moon, over the Valley of Aijalon." So the sun stood still, and the moon stopped, till the nation avenged itself on its enemies, as it is written in the Book of Jashar. The sun stopped in the middle of the sky and delayed going down about a full day. There has never been a day like it before or since, a day when the LORD listened to a human being. Surely the LORD was fighting for Israel!
>
> Joshua 10:12–14

Because God kept the sun from going down, Joshua and the Israelites won a great victory over their enemies.

In the battlespace we are currently in against the forces of darkness for the souls of men and women, can we not ask the Father for mighty miracles and victory for those who need Christ, for those who need a miracle and for those who need deliverance from sin? While we are fearful, for many reasons, to ask, the reality is that God is standing ready to work on our behalf and to intervene here on planet earth.

The Battlespace of the Mind

One of the big deceptions in the battlespace for the mind is the lie Satan tells us continually: "Did God really say you can move mountains? Come on, you know you can't do that," and "Look at your life. God could never use someone like you."

We are deceived continually by our enemy (as well as by our flesh) that we are only human, after all, and that God cannot expect us to see real miracles or use us to win the lost or deliver the oppressed. This is the lie or deception we must overcome in the name of Jesus.

Joshua was willing to ask big when it came time to ask God for something big. The question is: How big is our God, and is He able to deliver us from deception and evil in this day?

Jimmy Evans says the key to standing firm against the lies and seductions of the enemy is found in 2 Corinthians 10:3–5:

> For though we live in the world, we do not wage war as the world does. The weapons we fight with are not the weapons of the world. On the contrary, they have divine power to demolish strongholds. We demolish arguments and every pretension that sets itself up against the knowledge of God, and we take captive every thought to make it obedient to Christ.[6]

What does it mean to take every thought captive to obey Christ? Evans explains,

> Any thought that you don't take captive will take you captive. Any thought that you haven't taken captive has you captive. So when a thought comes into your mind, it says that it exalts itself above the knowledge of God.
>
> Every person who gets saved is, to some degree, in bondage mentally. You don't have the Word of God. The only thing that will set you free is the Word.
>
> Jesus said, "If you abide in my word, you are truly my disciples, and you will know the truth, and the truth will set you

185

free" (John 8:31–32 ESV). So when I come to Jesus, I begin to let the Word into my mind. "The Word of God is living and active, sharper than any two-edged sword" (Hebrews 4:12 ESV). You don't read the Bible. The Bible reads you. The Word of God is the only thing that keeps you from being deceived. It's the only thing that can set you free.[7]

When Evans and his wife got saved, he says, they went through a process of having to get set free from "all the crud that was on us" from growing up in homes where their parents weren't believers. And Evans returns to 2 Corinthians 10:3–5:

> It says taking "captive every thought." The word *captive* means "spearpoint." And the word *obedience* means "to listen under." So we're taking every thought in our minds like a threat—every thought that does not conform with the Word of God. I put a spear under its neck because it has me captive and I make it "listen under" Jesus. Every thought that agrees with Jesus can stay. Every thought that doesn't agree with Jesus has to leave. I reject it and replace it with the Word of God.
>
> You can't take a thought out of your mind, but you can replace it with the truth. The process of deception is the devil taking truth away from us—or we never had it in the first place. Our minds are full of deceiving thoughts, and this is the battlefield. That's for sure! But the process of freedom is, Get into the Word of God.[8]

TACTICS, TECHNIQUES AND PROCEDURES

How do you overcome the lies and deceptions of the enemy in the battlespace of the mind with the unshakable knowledge of Jesus?

1. **Ask God to show you** if there are any deceptions in your life and mind. If there are, commit to diving into the Word of God each day, perhaps in the morning before you begin your day. Set this time aside to let your mind be transformed by the living Word of God. If you do, you will begin to see the supernatural power of God unleashed in your life.

2. **Ask God to deliver you** from any deception or traps of the enemy. Satan and his demons are relentless, setting traps to lure you into sin, trying to weaken your walk with the Lord and presenting you with an endless array of deceptions to derail your God-ordained destiny. But you have the power of prayer at your disposal—the ability to ask the Lord God Almighty to help you see through the traps of the deceiver and triumph in truth.

3. **Ask God to help you** see how big He really is, and that, as for Joshua, He can go above and beyond anything you can imagine. God created the universe, earth, life—and you! If He can do that, He can surely "do immeasurably more than all we ask or imagine, according to his power that is at work within us" (Ephesians 3:20). The Lord God is the God of the impossible. Many saints and sinners throughout history have discovered this universal truth, experiencing the miraculous power of God. All He asks is that we believe and have faith.

4. **Ask God to open your eyes,** as Elisha prayed for his servant, to the supernatural events taking place around you. This does not mean you will see angels and demons under every bush. It does mean God will open your eyes and ears to the things you must see and hear. Who knows what incredible things the Lord will reveal to you?

14

Family and Society

If you really want to do something, you'll find a way. If you don't, you'll find an excuse.

JIM ROHN, American entrepreneur,
motivational speaker and author

EARLY 2002
FORT CAMPBELL MILITARY AND FAMILY SUPPORT CENTER
FORT CAMPBELL, KENTUCKY

It was a seemingly uneventful morning when a couple walked in for marriage relationship counseling. My secretary had them fill out the proper forms, then ushered them into my office. I began asking them the usual questions.

At first I did not detect anything out of the ordinary about this couple. Then I began to discern a certain vibe. Even so, nothing alarmed me until I asked one particular question: Are you two married to each other? The answer came back with a resounding no.

There are times in life when things go into slow motion. I do not know to this day all the thoughts I had or the questions I was going to ask, but alarm bells went off in my head.

They explained that the woman's husband had gone off to war as an infantryman with the 101st Airborne Division. This man had moved in with her while her husband was deployed. They wanted counseling to improve their relationship.

The first alarm bell went off inside of me as I pictured the husband coming back from war and finding this guy with his wife, and then committing double homicide. The second alarm bell went off inside of me warning me not to overreact.

Too late. I came unglued, which is both unprofessional and un-Christian. It got so bad that my usually calm secretary came bursting through the door. She said the building was literally shaking.

"Let me get this straight," I was bellowing to this couple. "You came in here for help in an adulterous relationship? Is that right? What part of this don't you get? Do you understand that when that husband returns from war, things are not going to be pretty?"

They left in a hurry. Soon afterward, the man, who was also a soldier, was separated from the U.S. Army on misconduct charges.

I learned a few things from this situation. First, I told myself, never assume you are dealing with a biblically rightful situation. Second, things do not always appear as they are. Third, when in doubt ask the right questions. And fourth, some people have no concept of right or wrong.

Families Under Attack

The family is the building block of society. Family is where we grow up learning how to interact with our world and what it means to be a member of the human race. God designed the family to be the model of unconditional love, a pillar of strength for family members in times of adversity and a joy-filled unit in times of peace and tranquility.

This model or template is found in the first book and first chapter of the Bible, Genesis 1:27–28 (NKJV):

> God created man in His own image; in the image of God He created him; male and female He created them. Then God blessed them, and God said to them, "Be fruitful and multiply; fill the earth and subdue it; have dominion over the fish of the sea, over the birds of the air, and over every living thing that moves on the earth."

In the times in which we live, the family is under attack from Satan. When the family structure and purpose are attacked, chaos and confusion occur. Deception about what a family is and how a family should operate is prevalent throughout the world.

Currently in America, the average marriage lasts a little more than eight years (8.2 years). The divorce rate in the U.S. hovers between forty and fifty percent of all marriages.[1]

The divorce rate among Christians is lower than that of the general population. A sociologist at the University of Connecticut found that sixty percent of people who identify as Christian but rarely attend church have been divorced, compared to 38 percent of those who attend church regularly.

Even so, the divorce rate among regular churchgoers is higher than it should be.[2] Why is that? Because the standards of churches have dropped over time; because there is less accountability; because preaching does not uphold biblical standards; because there is a lack of emphasis on strong families and religious affiliation; and because the family is under attack.

Interestingly, the Pew Research Center found that Protestants (those who identified as non-Catholic but Christian) had a divorce rate of about 51 percent out of a sampling of 4,752 individuals.[3]

Paul Pickern of All Pro Pastors International points out that many pastors, like many Christians, also have marriage problems:

> Pastors are so busy being pastors that they don't know what the enemy is doing out there. They are so busy that they can be insensitive. That's why pastors so often have marriage problems. They are trying to be good pastors, but they're not being good husbands; they're not being good dads. They are not taught that their first responsibility is still the family.
>
> This may sound odd, but when the Holy Spirit calls you to be a pastor, it doesn't change you from needing to be a good daddy to your children. Being a good pastor is in addition to that, not a replacement for that.
>
> Many pastors' marriages are struggling, but many, by God's grace, have married godly women who love the Lord, so they are staying with them. I personally see marriages that have no life in them because of the work of the ministry. It doesn't have to be that way.[4]

Lot's Poor Choice

It is no secret, then, that the order God set in motion for the family is coming unraveled. As I saw in my counseling appointment at Fort Campbell, what is abhorrent to God is now commonplace in the world. Let's go back to the book of Genesis and see what happens when we make poor choices and are influenced by the world's evil agenda.

When Abram and his nephew Lot decided to part company, since their herds of livestock were so vast that "the land could not support them" (Genesis 13:6), Abram gave Lot the choice of where to raise his family and his livestock:

> Abram said to Lot, "Please let there be no strife between you and me, and between my herdsmen and your herdsmen; for we

are brethren. Is not the whole land before you? Please separate from me. If you take the left, then I will go to the right; or, if you go to the right, then I will go to the left."

And Lot lifted his eyes and saw all the plain of Jordan, that it was well watered everywhere (before the LORD destroyed Sodom and Gomorrah) like the garden of the LORD, like the land of Egypt as you go toward Zoar. Then Lot chose for himself all the plain of Jordan, and Lot journeyed east. And they separated from each other.

verses 8–11 NKJV

Oh, Lot liked the way it looked. The whole plain of the Jordan "was well watered everywhere . . . like the garden of the LORD." But did he consider the eternal consequences of his decision? Perhaps he chose Sodom for the financial opportunities, or maybe for prestige, or it could be that it had the right schools for the kids. As head of his family, Lot was responsible to move them to the right place at the right time. Instead,

Lot dwelt in the cities of the plain and pitched his tent even as far as Sodom. But the men of Sodom were exceedingly wicked and sinful against the LORD.

verses 12–13 NKJV

When Lot selected Sodom as the place to live and raise his family, he made a poor choice. He knew better. He knew what he was getting into. That he "pitched his tent even as far as Sodom" would translate that he lived among the Sodomites and interacted with them, so much so that he became part of them. He became so steeped in that ungodly culture that when the angels of God were sent to rescue him from it, he refused to go.

When he hesitated, the men grasped his hand and the hands of his wife and of his two daughters and led them safely out

of the city, for the LORD was merciful to them. As soon as they
had brought them out, one of them said, "Flee for your lives!
Don't look back, and don't stop anywhere in the plain! Flee to
the mountains or you will be swept away!"

Genesis 19:16–17

The story of Sodom and Gomorrah is one of the most famous stories in history—the account of when God "rained
down burning sulfur on Sodom and Gomorrah" (Genesis
19:24), destroying the notoriously sinful cities because of their
wickedness. For centuries, however, critical scholars challenged
the account, arguing that the cities were merely legendary
places used by the biblical author to explain a moral metaphor.

Now, following fifteen years of excavations, Joseph M.
Holden, president of Veritas International University in Santa
Ana, California, says archaeologists have uncovered at Tall el-
Hamman—what some consider to have been Sodom near the
Dead Sea—a "massive destruction layer" at least three me-
ters thick containing the scattered, charred remains of people
"blown apart," melted pottery and other debris, indicating that
the area was "destroyed in a sudden, intense, high-heat catastrophic event" around 1800 to 1700 BC.[5]

The dig reveals that Middle Bronze Age pottery was heated
to 1,500–20,000 degrees Fahrenheit (volcanic lava, by compari-
son, is about 2,000 degrees Fahrenheit; while the sun burns
at about 7,000 degrees Fahrenheit), creating a "melting" phenomenon and glassy-appearing pottery like the trinitite ("desert glass") found at ground zero of the United States' nuclear
weapon testing area in New Mexico in the 1940s. Holden says
of this melting phenomenon,

> It certainly wasn't any fire or destruction that man can produce
> here on earth. Really, there is only one kind of naturally oc-
> curring phenomenon, and we've narrowed it down to a cosmic

193

airburst much like what happened in Tunguska, Russia, in 1908. There was considerable destruction. The walls were picked up and thrown off their foundations. This was no earthquake crumbling. This was the equivalent of a nuclear megaton explosion that rained fire and brimstone on the biblical city of Sodom, just as the Bible describes.[6]

Surprisingly, archaeological evidence also points to the truth of the story of Lot's wife being turned into a pillar of salt. One of the two angels had warned them, "Flee for your lives! Don't look back, and don't stop anywhere in the plain!" (Genesis 19:17).

But Lot's wife looked back, and she became a pillar of salt.

verse 26

Having been warned by the angels, was she turned into a pillar of salt just for looking back? No, the meaning of the phrase *looked back* is clear; she longed to go back to Sodom. Holden explains,

The Bible says that Lot's wife "looked back." *Looked back* in Hebrew doesn't mean a casual glance back. The context tells us she was dragging her feet and didn't want to leave.

She left reluctantly, dragging her feet, and her dragging her feet kept her in the blast radius too long. As the meteoritic airburst sped toward Sodom at low altitude over the Dead Sea, a massive explosion occurred about one kilometer in the sky, with frontal shockwaves that forced the super-heated brine and salt from the Dead Sea up onto the land. She was caught in that and probably got baked with the heat into that posture and form. So scientifically you can explain even that passage.

So destructive was the Sodom catastrophe that the entire southern Jordan Valley, along with its agricultural land and cities, was desolate for the next 700 years.[7]

The archaeological findings confirm that the biblical story is not a moral metaphor but an actual historical account serving as a warning for us not to be tainted by the world's evil agenda.

Like Abram's nephew Lot, we may not understand how tainted we are because the world infects us ever so slowly. Lot had a difficult time leaving that place because he may not have recognized how sin and deception had sneaked into his psyche. Deception creeps in as we become part of this ungodly world.

So we must be prayerful and vigilant in the choices we make in deciding where we will live, the friends we choose, the opportunities we take, the way we live and what it all means in light of heaven. Our lives and the lives of our families are at stake.

Fighting Deception in the Family

We have seen that the family in America and around the world is under attack, and for good reason. Our enemy, Satan, knows that if he can dismantle God's grand design, he can disrupt God's plan of redemption. You see, God created one man and one woman so that they may join as one, and work to have dominion over the earth. This design has balance, health and longevity. But the enemy wants to change the definition of *family* to fit his own wicked agenda.

The problem is, as seen throughout history, no nation can survive when wickedness reigns. The people of Sodom and Gomorrah had no clue that their very lifestyle would bring about the demise of their cities.

Rabbi Jonathan Cahn says America has been warned repeatedly of judgment unless people turn back and turn to God. Cahn, author of the bestselling *The Harbinger*, refers to the September 11, 2001, terrorist attacks on the United States:

> The pattern of judgment is that, after calling and calling and calling on the nation turning away, He allows it to be shaken. He

allows an enemy to make a strike on the land. That happened in ancient times, and it happened in modern times with America on 9/11. God allowed that. It was a shaking.

For those who know *The Harbinger*, that began at the time of the appearance of the nine harbingers of judgment, the same harbingers that appeared in ancient Israel. Well, now we are at the other end of this thing, so this is a crucial moment for America. Ancient Israel actually went away from God and never came back. America has been following that pattern, too. If we don't turn around—that's what *The Return* is—and have a change of course, we will head to judgment and calamity. We're already seeing the beginning of shakings.[8]

Fighting deception in our families is key to this return to God. Fighting deception in our families starts when we begin to value the family over everything else in our culture. We must start right now because if we wait until tomorrow, it may be too late.

It means that we spend time every day nurturing and caring for our spouse and children.

It means reading the Bible and praying with our kids daily; knowing what they are learning in school (if we are not home-schooling); correcting them lovingly; monitoring what they watch on television and on their media devices; knowing who their friends are; and taking them to church consistently to learn more of the Word of God.

It also means that we treat our spouses as deserving of admiration and respect; carefully listening to him or her; having a date night once a week; celebrating our anniversary every year; and investing in the relationship by reading the Word and praying together every day.

Military leadership has implemented ways to help support the family during war and long deployments. One of the best practices in the U.S. Army is Family Readiness Groups (now called Soldier and Family Readiness Groups). These groups form the basis for families of soldiers to support each other and their commanders. They have trained leaders who hold meetings to disseminate unit news, convey how the soldiers are doing and much more. It is a strong support system in times of war and separation.

One of the most difficult things I had to learn was praying with my wife every day. I was like many men who have a problem with that, because praying together opens up that intimate, spiritual part of us that we would rather not share.

Being stationed at Fort Benning, Georgia, at that time the home of the infantry, I found myself really enjoying the toughness and esprit de corps. I liked the "muddy boots" ministry of being out training with the soldiers. One time a platoon of lieutenants came by my house at Fort Benning early one morning and wanted me to join them on their eight-mile road march with full-fledged gear. This is the stuff I loved!

So when I received a call one day from the Pentagon asking if I would like to attend the family life course at Benning, earn a master of science in counseling and become a family life–trained chaplain, I was not interested. I had always told my wife that I wanted no part with those non–field duty chaplains who spent their day in the office drinking coffee.

But God had other plans for me, and I accepted the offer because I wanted to stabilize my family for another year at Benning.

Part of the course was spending a year being counseled by a professional. In that time, I learned more about myself from the reflections of a professional counselor. I learned more about who I was and how to be a better listener. I learned more about families and family systems and how they influence our society.

To this day Esther tells me that the course was the best thing that ever happened to me.

The truth is, all of us should understand the grand importance of family. It is the building block of society and the plan of God.

TACTICS, TECHNIQUES AND PROCEDURES

How do you navigate the pitfalls of deception when it comes to your marriage and your family?

1. **Read and study.** Make it a point to read and study the Bible about the importance of the family, and gather godly resources on how the family operates. Two such resources on the web are Focus on the Family and FamilyLife.

2. **Look hard at your schedule and calendar.** What does it tell you about the time you spend with your family? What can you change to align it with God's priorities in your life?

3. **If married,** are you praying and reading the Bible with your spouse every day? If not, start today. There are plenty of apps on reading the Bible through every year such as YouVersion, ReadScripture or Streetlights.

4. **If you have children,** spend time with them every day, and read the Word to them using the myriad of children's Bibles. There are Bibles for teens out there as well. Are you monitoring what your children are learning at school and on TV? Be vigilant because your adversary, the devil, is also monitoring your kids.

15

What Right Looks Like

There is a way that seems right to a man, but its end is the way of death.

PROVERBS 14:12 NKJV

WINTER 1990
43RD AIR DEFENSE ARTILLERY REGIMENT
FORT BLISS, TEXAS

"Chaplain, I need you to go out there and make this right. Get it fixed."

The commander has just given me an impossible task. We are deployed at Fort Bliss, Texas, for a 43rd Air Defense Artillery Regiment (Patriot) live fire exercise in the desert. Each of the Patriot antimissiles costs more than a million dollars, and there is no room for error since dignitaries will be observing.

There is one major problem. Bravo Battery's radar unit is inoperable, and the live fire exercise is fewer than twelve hours away. With no radar, no missile can be fired. The commander, desperate for a solution, has just ordered me to go out to Bravo Battery and pray for a miracle.

I direct my chaplain assistant to drive me out to the right location in the field. He looks at me as though I am crazy. "Sir, how in the world are we going to make this radar operational again?"

"We aren't," I reply, "but God is."

As we approach the Bravo Battery location in the middle of the desert, the battery commander greets us and briefs me on the situation. "Chaplain, we've been working on this radar with our best people, both military and civilian contractors. No good."

I understand the gravity of the situation and ask him to get his entire command out to the radar site.

"And what exactly are we going to do?" he asks.

"I'll let you know when we're assembled."

All Bravo Battery personnel gather out in front of the radar, and I direct them to hold hands as I lay my hands on the radar unit. Can you picture this in your mind?

"O God," I pray, "we need a miracle, and we humbly ask that You in Your mighty wisdom touch this radar and make it once again operational."

Nothing happens.

I return to the tactical operation center for another evening briefing with the commander and battalion staff. When my turn comes to speak at the staff meeting, the commander says, "Chaplain, your prayers are not worth [expletive]!"

I sink low in my chair.

Suddenly the tactical phone buzzes. The commander answers it, then puts it down quietly.

"Gentlemen," he says to the entire group, "the Bravo Battery radar is operational, and we'll have our live fire tomorrow morning."

The battalion staff erupts in applause and cheers. I am beaming and relieved both at the same time.

The commander smiles at me and says gruffly, "Chaplain, don't get too cocky."

I smile back at him.

After we return from the field the following morning from a successful missile launch, we celebrate with a formal affair called a dining-in, where the commander awards me with a homemade silver star to wear around my neck as a reminder of the time God intervened on our behalf.

What Is "Right"?

You hear this phrase all the time in the military: "This is what right looks like." You hear it first in basic training and on into the frontline maneuver units. The reason for the phrase is simple: If you do not do it right, it may cost you your life.

"Right" is defined in the manuals and tactical procedures that you learn over the years. For instance, you learn to ensure that your weapon is properly cleaned and cared for, because if it misfires in a firefight, it may cost your life and the lives of your fellow soldiers. You learn disciplines through practice and through what others have learned before you.

It is the same in the life of being a Christ-follower. We do not get to choose what is right just because it feels good, or because we *think* something is right. We learn through the Bible that God knows what He is talking about, even though we may not understand it. Trust His Word!

I learned a few things from that experience praying for the Bravo Battery's radar unit.

First and foremost, what right really looks like is that God is in control and we are not. This is His universe, His world, His creation and His Word. We are reflections of the glory of God. We are to trust Him for everything and then obey, even when we do not understand or when the culture is against us.

We can succumb to the world or we can bow to God. We cannot have it both ways.

Second, if we do not give up on God, He will not give up on us. The word is *perseverance*. God wants us to lean on Him when we do not know what to do or understand what is going on.

Like now! With the world in upheaval and turmoil, with plagues, earthquakes, fires and floods all around, it is hard to figure out what is really going on, but we have to continue on in God.

Finally, I could have told the commander that God does not do miracles in this day and age. I could have given in to my fear of looking stupid in front of those soldiers. Or I could have disobeyed the commander's orders and not prayed. But I knew what right really looks like, and it is this: God is still in the miracle-working business. I knew what right looked like because I believed the Word of God that says, "You may ask me for anything in my name, and I will do it" (John 14:14). I was definitely asking!

The great deception in our time is that God, if He even exists, is far off and does not care about this tiny little planet in the midst of a vast universe.

It reminds me of the time in the Bible when "everyone did what was right in his own eyes" (Judges 17:6 NKJV). In the period of the judges, after the deaths of Moses and Joshua, the Jews had no king or leader and did whatever pleased them.

In the same way, if there is no God, we can do whatever we want, however we want. If there is a God, on the other hand, we must keep in step and in tune with His will as written in His Word.

Jimmy Evans says,

> The apostle Paul in 2 Thessalonians 2:1–12 says that the primary sign of the end times is a great falling away from the truth.

Today the greatest lie in the world is the lie of humanism—that man doesn't need God; that he can save himself. Our schools have become very humanistic. Even a lot of religious institutions are more focused on people than on God. Romans 1:25 says that ungodly people "worshiped and served the creature rather than the Creator" (NKJV). I believe the greatest deception of all is that we don't need God.[1]

Three Lessons from Scripture

It is important that we engage our culture outside the four walls of the church and speak the Word wherever we are, at work or at home or just out and about. And we must translate our church language into the everyday language of the common person.

People of our day and culture who do not believe in Jesus Christ do not think like believers or share our Christian worldview. They are blinded by the "god of this age" (2 Corinthians 4:4). They do not know what right looks like; we need to show them the way. We need to "reason" with them.

Let's look at three Bible characters and how they communicated in their own cultures.

Paul and a New Worldview

While the apostle Paul was waiting for Silas and Timothy in Athens, he encountered Stoic and Epicurean philosophers who spent all their time debating and learning about new ideas and religions.

> He was greatly distressed to see that the city was full of idols. So he reasoned in the synagogue with both Jews and God-fearing Greeks, as well as in the marketplace day by day with those who happened to be there.
>
> Acts 17:16–17

Here Paul came face-to-face with people of a far different culture and worldview. He did not handle this situation as if they were Jews in a synagogue; no, he reasoned with them in their own way of thinking:

> Paul then stood up in the meeting of the Areopagus and said: "People of Athens! I see that in every way you are very religious. For as I walked around and looked carefully at your objects of worship, I even found an altar with this inscription: TO AN UNKNOWN GOD. So you are ignorant of the very thing you worship—and this is what I am going to proclaim to you."
>
> verses 22–23

Some "sneered" (verse 32), but others were intensely interested in what Paul had to say.

It is important to note that Paul shared his faith not only on the Sabbath (our Sunday) in the synagogue but also in the marketplace and the workplace. He engaged his faith every day.

Moses and the Bronze Serpent

Sometimes not doing what is right leads to suffering, as happened with the children of Israel in the desert:

> They traveled from Mount Hor along the route to the Red Sea, to go around Edom. But the people grew impatient on the way; they spoke against God and against Moses, and said: "Why have you brought us up out of Egypt to die in the wilderness? There is no bread! There is no water! And we detest this miserable food!"
>
> Then the LORD sent venomous snakes among them; they bit the people and many Israelites died. The people came to Moses and said, "We sinned when we spoke against the LORD and against you. Pray that the LORD will take the snakes away from us." So Moses prayed for the people.
>
> The LORD said to Moses, "Make a snake and put it up on a pole; anyone who is bitten can look at it and live." So Moses

made a bronze snake and put it up on a pole. Then when anyone was bitten by a snake and looked at the bronze snake, they lived.

Numbers 21:4–9

The lesson is both simple and complex. Simple, because the Israelites knew God hated complaining, moaning and griping, yet they did it anyway. They knew what right looked like but refused to obey—until suffering came their way.

Sometimes it takes the bite of a snake in our lives to shake us into reality and help us understand that this life can be difficult, trying and perplexing, but that God is supremely orchestrating a divine concert in our lives to bring us to the ultimate eternal home where there is no pain or sorrow.

Complex, because how was Moses to believe that the complaining people could be healed just by looking at a bronze snake lifted up? He could have said, "No way can a snake, the enemy of old, be lifted up and bring divine healing to the population." God did not explain to Moses the how and why; He simply asked him to believe and carry out the mission.

Deception occurs in our lives as Christ-followers when we fail to believe God. He may tell us to do something that makes no sense. If we do not obey, we are telling God that we know more than He does or that our ways our higher than His. Then deception creeps slowly into different areas of life until we no longer hear the voice of God or heed His commands.

Those Israelites in the desert who were complaining against Moses and God found out the hard way that it does not pay to undermine God or His leaders who are put into positions of authority over us.

Jeremiah, that great prophet of old, stated that "the heart is deceitful above all things and beyond cure. Who can understand it?" (Jeremiah 17:9). God knows and understands the heart when we do not. This is why we must trust Him even when we do not understand.

Jeremiah in the Cistern

The story of how the prophet Jeremiah was placed in a deep well full of mud offers another valuable lesson—this one on when doing right leads to suffering. It happened when Judah was on the verge of being captured by Babylon, and certain leaders objected to Jeremiah's message. He prophesied

> "This is what the LORD says: 'Whoever stays in this city will die by the sword, famine or plague, but whoever goes over to the Babylonians will live. They will escape with their lives; they will live.' And this is what the LORD says: 'This city will certainly be given into the hands of the army of the king of Babylon, who will capture it.'"
>
> Then the officials said to the king, "This man should be put to death. He is discouraging the soldiers who are left in this city, as well as all the people, by the things he is saying to them. This man is not seeking the good of these people but their ruin."
>
> "He is in your hands," King Zedekiah answered. "The king can do nothing to oppose you."
>
> So they took Jeremiah and put him into the cistern of Malkijah, the king's son, which was in the courtyard of the guard. They lowered Jeremiah by ropes into the cistern; it had no water in it, only mud, and Jeremiah sank down into the mud.
>
> Jeremiah 38:2–6

There may come a time in your life when you proclaim the Lord's word faithfully to fellow workers or even strangers, and you are persecuted for your faith. Do not be discouraged but rejoice in the fact that the Lord counts you worthy. Jeremiah was speaking the word of the Lord faithfully and was thrown into the depths of a muddy well, left to die.

He could have given up his trust in God then and there, but he did not because he knew that the One who sent him spoke the truth and was faithful. Jeremiah knew what right looked like.

He was rescued from the cistern and served out his time in the king's courtyard of the guard. He had the eternal perspective.

TACTICS, TECHNIQUES AND PROCEDURES

Military people study manuals to understand the right way of doing things, passed on by generations of those who have gone through many wars and battles. Here are some of those principles that can change your life:

1. **Look at your past.** Review your past and see if you have learned from your mistakes. Were there times you thought you were doing the right thing but found out differently? What were they, and how did you correct those errors?

2. **Find a strong, trusted, believing mentor.** Be vulnerable in sharing, and ask him or her to point out some of your mistakes and flaws. Ask what right looks like from that person's worldview and perspective.

3. **Take a close look at your church.** Is it challenging your walk with the Lord? If it is, how so? If it is not, is it time to rethink your direction? Remember, you may be there to be an influencer, so ask God for guidance.

4. **Evaluate your life.** Is there one thing you can change? What is it? And why is it not happening now?

16

Avoiding End-Times Pitfalls

The arrogant have dug pits for me, people who are not in accord with Your Law.

PSALM 119:85 NASB

WINTER 2002
GEORGIA NATIONAL GUARD INFANTRY, NORTH GEORGIA
NIGHT

My son, David Micah Giammona, is in a Georgia National Guard infantry long-range surveillance detachment executing night land-navigation training in the mountains of north Georgia. He is following his team leader, who is just ahead. It is pitch-black. The only thing he can see is the illuminated "cat eyes" on the back of the sergeant's patrol cap.

Suddenly those cat eyes disappear. Micah stops in his tracks, unsure of what has just happened. He hears a crash and then some moaning, but it sounds far away. Something has gone terribly wrong.

208

When he turns on his flashlight, he finds the reason his team leader has disappeared. There is no ground in front of him. The sergeant has fallen into a deep twelve-to-fifteen-foot pit. Micah would have been next, except that he stopped short and turned on some light.

Micah calls for a medic and starts emergency procedures to get his team leader out of the pit.

The Pits

Fortunately, that team leader survived to live another day. After dropping twelve to fifteen feet, he injured his back and broke his wrist. If Micah had not stopped and turned on his flashlight, he also would have fallen into the pit.

It seems that a whole lineup of biblical characters ended up in pits of one form or another—not only Joseph, thrown into a pit and sold into slavery, but Jeremiah thrown into a muddy well (which we looked at in the last chapter); Daniel thrown into the lions' den; Shadrach, Meshach and Abednego thrown into a fiery furnace; Jonah swallowed up in the belly of a great fish; and Paul and Silas thrown into a dungeon.

A pit is a dark, nasty thing. To fall into one is not a pleasant experience. Just ask Joseph. After his brothers threw him into an empty cistern, they sold him to the Ishmaelites for twenty shekels of silver (see Genesis 37:23–28). Joseph learned a few lessons in that pit, in Potiphar's house and in the Egyptian prison. He learned over time to trust in God and God's timing.

Another man of God learned a hard lesson about the importance of doing God's will. Jonah kept going *down* when he ran from God. He went *down* to Joppa:

The word of the LORD came to Jonah the son of Amittai, saying, "Arise, go to Nineveh, that great city, and cry out against it; for their wickedness has come up before Me." But Jonah arose to flee to Tarshish from the presence of the Lord. He went down to Joppa. . . .

Jonah 1:1–3 NKJV

and then went *down* into the ship:

> . . . and found a ship going to Tarshish; so he paid the fare, and went down into it, to go with them to Tarshish from the presence of the Lord.

verse 3

and then went *down* into the sea:

> So they picked up Jonah and threw him into the sea, and the sea ceased from its raging. Then the men feared the Lord exceedingly, and offered a sacrifice to the Lord and took vows.

verses 15–16

and then went *down* into the belly of a great fish:

> Now the Lord had prepared a great fish to swallow Jonah. And Jonah was in the belly of the fish three days and three nights.

verse 17

Only when he repented of his sin of rebellion and praised God did the great fish "[vomit] Jonah onto dry land" (Jonah 2:10).

Jonah, who went on to obey God and preach to Nineveh, could have avoided all this if he had only followed the light or the word of the Lord. Instead, he chose rebellion and darkness.

Light

To avoid pitfalls, you need light. Plenty of scriptural examples show us the way. For example, Proverbs 6:23 (BSB) tells us: "This commandment is a lamp, this teaching is a light, and the re-proofs of discipline are the way to life."

Peter offers this instruction:

> We also have the word of the prophets as confirmed beyond doubt. And you will do well to pay attention to it, as to a lamp shining in a dark place, until the day dawns and the morning star rises in your hearts.
>
> 2 Peter 1:19 BSB

Illumination from the Word of God has always been the means by which believers navigate dark times. We live in such times right now. Chaos and confusion reign supreme, and things will only continue to spiral down until the coming of the Lord. Notice that when the Lord returns, darkness will prevail:

> Behold, the Day of the LORD is coming—cruel, with fury and burning anger—to make the earth a desolation and to destroy the sinners within it. For the stars of heaven and their constellations will not give their light. The rising sun will be darkened, and the moon will not give its light.
>
> Isaiah 13:9–10 BSB

But light is available to all who are followers of Christ, even in the darkest of times. The issue is, are you going to follow the light or the darkness?

We have noted throughout this book the apostle Paul's prophecy in 2 Thessalonians 2 that many believers will fall away in the great apostasy and follow the Antichrist when he is revealed. Remember, he is the entity who imitates Christ in almost every way. He will be resurrected from the dead (Revelation 13:3 says he suffers a fatal wound but is healed); he will perform miracles; and he will proclaim himself to be God. This is the reason millions will follow him: They will think he is the Christ. Satan always tries to mimic God.

Listen once again to Paul's warning of the deception of the "lawless one":

> The secret power of lawlessness is already at work; but the one who now holds it back will continue to do so till he is taken out of the way. And then the lawless one will be revealed, whom the Lord Jesus will overthrow with the breath of his mouth and destroy by the splendor of his coming. The coming of the lawless one will be in accordance with how Satan works. He will use all sorts of displays of power through signs and wonders that serve the lie, and all the ways that wickedness deceives those who are perishing. They perish because they refused to love the truth and so be saved. For this reason God sends them a powerful delusion so that they will believe the lie and so that all will be condemned who have not believed the truth but have delighted in wickedness.
>
> 2 Thessalonians 2:7–12

Only those with their spiritual lights turned on will survive the delusion and deception of the Antichrist. His lies and deception will be destroyed by "the splendor of [Christ's] coming" (verse 8). That splendor is His glory and brightness that no demon, devil or wicked human can look at and survive.

Paul and the Light

Paul himself was blinded by the light of the glory of God on his way to persecute believers in Damascus:

> Saul was still breathing out murderous threats against the Lord's disciples. He went to the high priest and asked him for letters to the synagogues in Damascus, so that if he found any there who belonged to the Way, whether men or women, he might

take them as prisoners to Jerusalem. As he neared Damascus on his journey, suddenly a light from heaven flashed around him. He fell to the ground and heard a voice say to him, "Saul, Saul, why do you persecute me?"

"Who are you, Lord?" Saul asked.

"I am Jesus, whom you are persecuting," he replied. "Now get up and go into the city, and you will be told what you must do."

Acts 9:1–6

Light from heaven is blinding to the lost and comforting to the saved. Paul was blinded by this light. Our world and our culture cannot bear the light; it is blinding to them because they are perishing. If they turn to God, then that very light will lead them to the truth.

Several years after Saul's conversion, when he and Silas had been flogged, put into chains and thrown into the dungeon, they worshiped God at midnight in the dark, even in their pain. Suddenly the very foundations of that prison were shaken:

About midnight Paul and Silas were praying and singing hymns to God, and the other prisoners were listening to them. Suddenly there was such a violent earthquake that the foundations of the prison were shaken. At once all the prison doors flew open, and everyone's chains came loose. The jailer woke up, and when he saw the prison doors open, he drew his sword and was about to kill himself because he thought the prisoners had escaped. But Paul shouted, "Don't harm yourself! We are all here!" The jailer called for lights, rushed in and fell trembling before Paul and Silas. He then brought them out and asked, "Sirs, what must I do to be saved?"

Acts 16:25–30

When God shakes this world—and He will—two things will happen. The rebellious will keep on rebelling, and the repentant will fall on their knees before God.

When "the jailer called for lights," it was symbolic of what was happening in himself and in the prison. God had shaken the place, and now spiritual light was shining into the lives of the jailer and his family.

Call for the light of the glorious Gospel to shine into your life and change you from the inside out. Call for the lamp of the Lord to guide you through these tumultuous times.

Rabbi Jonathan Bernis of Jewish Voice Ministries International says that avoiding the pitfalls of deception in the end times requires believers to "see through the eyes of the Spirit, having ears to hear and eyes to see." He explains,

> This means we need to spend more time in the Good News than listening to the news. We need to be like the children of Issachar in 1 Chronicles 12:32, the generation who understood the times. I don't think the majority of Christians understand the times. We're ripping ourselves apart right now. The church is being polarized and sucked into political things. I'm not saying we shouldn't take a position. I'm saying that our dominant position should be based on seeing things through spiritual eyes and the Kingdom of God.
>
> I'm troubled by the lack of clarity about the times we live in. Nor do I see the coronavirus pandemic or suffering as something unique to our generation. What did we sign up for, right? I feel like I signed up for something different than I'm hearing most Christians feel they signed up for.
>
> As a Jew contemplating Jesus forty years ago, I read that I would be hated. I read that I would be persecuted. I read that there would be hard times and that I might lose my family over the direction I'm going. I don't understand why Christians are so surprised and asking, "Where is God?"
>
> I have unanswered whys, but I signed up for battle, and I think there's more ahead.[1]

Pitfalls

There are many deceptive pits to fall into during these end times. Let's take a look at some of them.

The Ostrich Syndrome

One of the great dangers to fall into is burying your head in the sand and pretending all is well. This is called the ostrich syndrome—although it turns out that ostriches do not bury their heads in the sand when danger approaches. They are just checking on their nest of eggs.

Some pastors and churches we know do not speak about the end times (or some other relevant topics) because it may generate fear in their congregations and chase away those checking out their churches for the first time. Many believers and their leaders are hoping things get back to "normal" so they can live in peace. (What is normal in this day and age is anyone's guess.)

"I think pastors who refuse to talk about the end times and prepare their people for the end times are guilty of spiritual malpractice," says Dr. Robert Jeffress, senior pastor of First Baptist Church in Dallas. He goes on:

> The book of Revelation is the only book in the entire Bible that has a special blessing associated with those who not only read it and hear it, but those who apply it. People wonder, "What relationship do the end times have with me today? I'm not nearly as concerned about the beast in Revelation as the beast I have to go to work for every day, Monday through Friday. What if the end times don't come for decades or centuries?"[2]

Answering these questions, Jeffress recalls the time he was serving as a Fox News contributor and a friend of his, the late Alan Colmes, a liberal political commentator for Fox, asked him if he believed he would live to see the return of Jesus Christ.

I said, "Alan, honestly, I don't know, but it really doesn't make any difference." He said, "What do you mean?" I said, "I'm 55 years old, and in the next thirty years or so, either He's coming or I'm going. But the end is near for me, and it is for you as well."

We need to be equipped for the end times—either for the end of the age or the end of our own lives. One way or the other, we're going to stand before God and give an account of our lives, and we had better be prepared.[3]

The Scripture tells us that in the end, people will be crying out for rocks to fall on them because they are afraid of Him who has returned to judge the earth:

> They said to the mountains and to the rocks, "Fall on us and hide us from the face of the one seated on the throne and from the wrath of the Lamb."
>
> Revelation 6:16 CSB

To avoid the deception of the ostrich syndrome, we need courage living in the end times. Valid spiritual and physical preparation is the key to navigate these uncharted waters. Ignore this fact at your own peril. It is critical to be in the know of world events, the Bible and its application to everyday living.

Self-Pity, Doubt and Fear

Another deceptive pit we can fall into during these end times is the pit of self-pity, doubt and fear. This can happen when we watch the news 24/7 and then throw our hands up in despair. Saturating ourselves with constant negative news is never a good thing. Many, out of fear, will end up following the culture and eventually the Antichrist.

We can face fear of the future, fear of the unknown, fear of death and a host of other fears that are real yet full of unbelief. Trust in politics, science, media, medicine, pastors and leaders may at times help us, but at other times will let us down. The question we need to ask ourselves is this: In whom do I put my trust—other people, Satan or God? Proverbs 3:5–6 tells us:

> Trust in the LORD with all your heart and lean not on your own understanding; in all your ways submit to him, and he will make your paths straight.

Yes, our trust is in the only One who can lead us in the right path.

Self-Preservation

The last pit we will talk about here—but not the last pit we can fall into—is the deception of self-preservation. This is a difficult one, to be sure, since God wired us not to want to jump off tall buildings or wrestle hippos.

There may come a time, however, when we will need to choose whom to follow. Some will choose to follow the path of least resistance or the easy way that leads to eternal loss.

If we follow Christ on the narrow road, it is sometimes a dangerous path in the eyes of the world. Whatever made Jim Elliot, one of five martyred missionaries in the 1950s to the indigenous Amazonian tribe in Ecuador (then known as the Aucas, now known as the Waodani), willing to give up his life for the cause of Christ? Jim and the four other missionaries knew that going into that tribal region could cost them their lives. They chose not to use pistols to defend themselves from being speared to death.

Why were he and his four friends willing to give up their lives for the cause of Christ? They had come to win the lost. This is what Elliot wrote: "He is no fool who gives what he cannot keep to gain that which he cannot lose."[4]

And many in the Waodani tribe came to saving faith in Jesus Christ.

There is an interesting sidenote to my son's story at the beginning of this chapter. The team leader who fell into the pit had warned his soldiers before going out that night to be careful about falling into a pit.

The most careful planning, prudence and preparation do not mean bad things cannot happen. After all we do, we need to trust God in every situation.

TACTICS, TECHNIQUES AND PROCEDURES

What are some ways to avoid end-times pitfalls?

1. **Turn off the TV and social media.** Instead, take a day and listen to the Lord. Find a safe, quiet space, even a large closet, to hide yourself away from all distractions. Listen to soft Christian music. And take time alone with the Lord.

2. **Do a Bible study** on all the biblical figures who found themselves in a pit or difficult situation. How did they fare? Did God deliver them all? Were some not spared? As a start, use the Scriptures found in this chapter.

3. **Consider what pit you fell into lately.** Are you still in one now? Has God helped you out of pits in the past? How did He do that?

4. **Get with a trusted Christian friend or mentor.** Discuss the theme of this chapter with him or her. What might you do to avoid pitfalls in your own life and journey?

Conclusion

Be One of the Few

Small is the gate and narrow the road that leads to life, and
only a few find it.

MATTHEW 7:14

Few recruiting slogans are as iconic as that of the United States
Marine Corps: *The Few. The Proud. The Marines.*

There is a reason the Marines selected that slogan: It is true.
The Marines have never looked for the majority to fill their
ranks; they want a select few worthy of the title *Marine.*

Life in all aspects is about choices and discernment. Those of
us who are serving or who have served in the military have gone
through some tough training that weeds out those who cannot
make the cut. The reason there are some very difficult courses in
the military—such as Army Ranger, Marine Force Recon and
Navy SEAL training—is that those branches are looking for the
best of the best. Only a select few graduate from those courses,
and it is meant to be that way. The military discriminates based
on performance, so that when service personnel are deployed
to war, they can win the battle.

219

In today's culture, by contrast, everybody is a winner, and there are no losers. If we raise our kids that way, they are in for a tough time the first time they fail to make the cut for a baseball team or a particular school or a job.

Unfortunately, even in the spiritual world, there are those who will enter the narrow gate to eternal life and those who will not. Jesus said,

> "Enter through the narrow gate. For wide is the gate and broad is the road that leads to destruction, and many enter through it. But small is the gate and narrow the road that leads to life, and only a few find it."

Matthew 7:13–14

In other words, many will not make the cut to eternal life. The main reason for that is deception. As the apostle Paul told the Corinthian church,

> The god of this age has blinded the minds of unbelievers, so that they cannot see the light of the gospel that displays the glory of Christ, who is the image of God.

2 Corinthians 4:4

And as for the very end? Revelation 12:9 tells us,

> The great dragon was hurled down—that ancient serpent called the devil, or Satan, who leads the whole world astray. He was hurled to the earth, and his angels with him.

As for those who worship the beast,

> All who dwell on earth will worship it, everyone whose name has not been written before the foundation of the world in the book of life of the Lamb who was slain.

Revelation 13:8 ESV

Let's not be in that majority who are not followers of the Lord. Let's be of the select few to enter the glory of heaven. We want to be on the winning team as followers of Christ.

As days get more and more difficult, we must realize that this present life is not all there is. To be one of the few, we cannot consider life so dear, and hold onto it so tightly, that we are willing to sacrifice our immortal future for a safe and comfortable present.

This life is only the beginning of life compared to all eternity. Paul stated, "I consider that our present sufferings are not worth comparing with the glory that will be revealed in us" (Romans 8:18). This was the mindset of the apostles of the Lord Jesus Christ. All of them were martyred for their faith except one, John, who wrote the book of Revelation. According to Tertullian, he was boiled in oil by the Romans, and when they could not kill him, they exiled him to the island of Patmos.[1]

Millions of believers over the centuries have been martyred for the faith because they were "looking forward to the city that has foundations, whose designer and builder is God" (Hebrews 11:10 ESV). We call this having an eternal worldview mindset.

When describing how we should live in these end times, the writer to the Hebrews said it best:

> Since we are surrounded by such a great cloud of witnesses, let us throw off everything that hinders and the sin that so easily entangles. And let us run with perseverance the race marked out for us, fixing our eyes on Jesus, the pioneer and perfecter of faith. For the joy set before him he endured the cross, scorning its shame, and sat down at the right hand of the throne of God. Consider him who endured such opposition from sinners, so that you will not grow weary and lose heart.
>
> Hebrews 12:1–3

Notes

Chapter 1 Complacency Can Kill You

1. Sun Tzu, *The Art of War* (Leicester, England: Allandale Online Publishing, 2000), 3, https://sites.ualberta.ca/~enoch/Readings/The_Art_Of_War.pdf.
2. Greg Laurie, April 13, 2021, telephone interview with Troy Anderson.
3. Paul McGuire, May 29, 2021, telephone interview with Troy Anderson.

Chapter 2 The Great Rebellion

1. Col. Peter Brzezinski, July 20, 2021, telephone interview with Troy Anderson.
2. Charles Snow, "What Is Cancel Culture and What Does It Have to Do with the SPLC?" Alliance Defending Freedom, November 19, 2019, https://adflegal.org/blog/what-cancel-culture-and-what-does-it-have-do-splc?sourcecode=10016058_r500&utm_source=grant&utm_medium=ppc&utm_campaign=Blog&gclid=Cj0KCQjw2tCGBhCLARIsABJGmZ7b8kgYQ_V9oIaZZrzeoB75dlxRYzxO-mjKW51Jq3cQWbV3J-f62T0aAm7YEALw_wcB.
3. Alex Newman, "Frankfurt School Weaponized US Education Against Civilization," *The Epoch Times*, updated March 10, 2020, https://www.theepochtimes.com/frankfurt-school-weaponized-u-s-education-against-civilization_3137064.html.
4. Mark R. Levin, *American Marxism* (New York: Simon & Schuster, 2021), 3, 12.
5. McGuire, May 29, 2021.
6. Jimmy Evans, September 22, 2021, Zoom interview with Col. David Giammona and Troy Anderson.

7. Rex Butler, "'Swear by the genius of our lord the emperor': False Worship and Persecution of Christians," New Orleans Baptist Theological Seminary, October 17, 2016, https://nobts.edu/geauxtherefore/articles/2016/swear-by-the-genius-of-our-lord-the-emperor--false-worship-and-persecution-of-christians.html.

8. Dr. Robert Jeffress, July 30, 2021, Zoom interview with Col. David Giammona and Troy Anderson.

9. Rabbi Jonathan Cahn, July 30, 2020, Skype interview with Troy Anderson.

10. Ibid.

11. Michael Gryboski, "Only 6% of Americans have a 'biblical worldview,' research from George Barna finds," *The Christian Post*, May 26, 2021, https://www.christianpost.com/news/only-6-of-americans-have-a-biblical-worldview-survey.html.

12. George Barna, "American Worldview Inventory 2021, Release #4: The National Religious Realignment," Arizona Christian University Cultural Research Center, June 8, 2021, https://www.arizonachristian.edu/wp-content/uploads/2021/06/CRC_AWVI2021_Release04_Digital_01_20210608.pdf.

13. Ibid.

Chapter 3 Subversion

1. Joint Chiefs of Staff, "Joint Doctrine Note 1–18 Strategy," 9, 13, April 25, 2018, https://www.jcs.mil/Portals/36/Documents/Doctrine/jdn_jg/jdn1_18.pdf.

2. Department of Defense, "Dictionary of Military and Associated Terms," http://www.dtic.mil/doctrine/dod_dictionary/data/s/7348.html.

3. J. Michael Waller, "Understanding Subversion: Considerations for our special operations forces," September 14, 2016, paper and lecture delivered at the John F. Kennedy Special Warfare Center, Fort Bragg, NC, https://www.linkedin.com/pulse/understanding-subversion-considerations-our-special-forces-waller.

4. Barna Group, "What Do Americans Believe About Jesus? 5 Popular Beliefs," April 1, 2015, https://www.barna.com/research/what-do-americans-believe-about-jesus-5-popular-beliefs/.

5. Rob Bell, *Love Wins: A Book about Heaven, Hell, and the Fate of Every Person Who Ever Lived* (New York: HarperOne, 2011), viii.

6. CBN News Staff, "Rob Bell Suggests Bible Not Relevant to Today's Culture," CBN News, February 19, 2015, https://www1.cbn.com/cbnnews/us/2015/february/rob-bell-suggests-bible-not-relevant-to-todays-culture.

7. Barack Obama, "Today is a big step in our march toward equality. Gay and lesbian couples now have the right to marry, just like anyone else. #LoveWins," Twitter, June 26, 2015, https://twitter.com/potus44/status/614435467120001024?lang=en.

8. The Rev. Kevin Jessip, June 12, 2021, in-person interview in Orlando, Florida, with Troy Anderson.

9. Ibid.

Chapter 4 Opposing Forces

1. Joint Chiefs of Staff, "Military Deception," Joint Publication 3-13.4, ix, Joint Chiefs of Staff, January 26, 2012, https://jfsc.ndu.edu/Portals/72/Documents/JC2IOS/Additional_Reading/1C3-JP_3-13-4_MILDEC.pdf.

2. Paul Pickern, July 19, 2021, telephone interview with Troy Anderson.

3. Lucas Miles, July 15, 2021, telephone interview with Troy Anderson.

4. McGuire, May 29, 2021.

5. Department of the Army, "Operations Security," Army Regulation 530-1, 10, September 26, 2014, https://fas.org/irp/doddir/army/ar530-1.pdf.

6. Sinclair Ferguson, "What Is Discernment?" Ligonier Ministries, May 8, 2020, https://www.ligonier.org/blog/discernment-thinking-gods-thoughts/.

7. Jerry Moses, July 16, 2021, telephone interview with Troy Anderson.

8. Mario Murillo quoted in Stephen Strang, "Mario Murillo Says Post-Election Church Must 'Find Its Moral Spine,' 'Get to the Bottom of Corruption,'" *Charisma*, December 2020, https://www.charismamag.com/blogs/the-strang-report/47326-mario-murillo-says-post-election-church-must-find-its-moral-spine-get-to-the-bottom-of-corruption.

9. Ibid.

Chapter 5 Psychological Operations

1. U.S. Army *Field Manual*, "Psychological Operations: Tactics, Techniques, and Procedures," page 11, Department of the Army, December 31, 2003, https://fas.org/irp/doddir/army/fm3-05-301.pdf.

2. U.S. Army *Field Manual*, "Psychological Operations: Tactics, Techniques, and Procedures," page 1-1, Department of the Army, October 28, 2005, https://fas.org/irp/doddir/army/fm3-05-302.pdf.

3. Lucas Miles, July 15, 2021, telephone interview with Troy Anderson.

4. Coco Perez, January 14, 2022, email interview with Col. David Giammona.

5. Impact 360 Institute, "Os Guinness on Faith, Politics, & Culture," https://www.impact360institute.org/articles/os-guinness-on-faith-politics-culture.

6. Barna Group Organization, "Tracking the Growth and Decline of Religious Segments: The Rise of Atheism, January 14, 2020, Barna, https://www.barna.com/rise-of-atheism.

7. CBN.com staff, "Wicca: What's the Fascination?" CBN.com, https://www1.cbn.com/books/wicca%3A-what%27s-the-fascination%3F.

8. Michael Lipka and Conrad Hackett, "Why Muslims are the world's fastest-growing religious group," Pew Research Center, April 6, 2017, https://

www.pewresearch.org/fact-tank/2017/04/06/why-muslims-are-the-worlds
-fastest-growing-religious-group.

9. The Church of England, "The Apostles' Creed," https://www.church
ofengland.org/our-faith/what-we-believe/apostles-creed.

10. Joint Chiefs of Staff, "Joint Publication 3-13.4 Military Deception,"
January 26, 2021, https://jfsc.ndu.edu/Portals/72/Documents/JC2IOS/Ad-
ditional_Reading/1C3-JP_3-13-4_MILDEC.pdf.

Chapter 6 Center of Operations

1. Dr. Senta German, "Ziggurat of Ur," Smarthistory, August 8, 2015,
accessed November 29, 2021, https://smarthistory.org/ziggurat-of-ur/.

2. Tim LaHaye and Ed Hindson, *The Popular Encyclopedia of Bible
Prophecy* (Eugene, Ore.: Harvest House, 2004), 23–27.

3. Brzezinski, July 20, 2021.

4. *Britannica*, s. v., "Temple of Jerusalem" by the editors of *Encyclopaedia
Britannica*, accessed July 29, 2021.

5. *Britannica*, s. v., "Temple of Jerusalem" by the editors of *Encyclopaedia
Britannica*, accessed July 30, 2021.

6. World Economic Forum, "The Great Reset," September 24, 2020,
https://www.weforum.org/great-reset/.

7. Donna Howell and Allie Henson, *Dark Covenant: How the Masses are
Being Groomed to Embrace the Unthinkable While the Leaders of Organized
Religion Make a Deal with the Devil* (Crane, Mo.: Defender, 2021), 31.

8. Ibid., 38.

9. Brzezinski, July 20, 2021.

10. Rabbi Jonathan Bernis, October 22, 2021, Zoom interview with Col.
David Giammona and Troy Anderson.

11. Christian Widener, *The Temple Revealed: The True Location of the
Jewish Temple Hidden in Plain Sight* (Rapid City, S. Dak.: End Times Berean,
2020), 21.

12. Michael J. Vlach, "Various Forms of Replacement Theology," spring
2009, The Masters Seminary, https://www.tms.edu/m/tmsj20d.pdf.

Chapter 7 Night-Vision Goggles

1. Jeffress, July 30, 2021.

2. Brittanica.com, https://www.britannica.com/topic/critical-race-theory.

3. Derrick A. Bell, "Who's Afraid of Critical Race Theory?" University of
Illinois Law Review, Vol. 1995, No. 4 (1995): 893, https://sph.umd.edu/sites
/default/files/files/Bell_Whos%20Afraid%20of%20CRT_1995UIllLRev893
.pdf (accessed December 3, 2020).

4. Jonathan Butcher, "Feeling Guilty About Everything? Thank Critical
Race Theory," The Heritage Foundation, December 7, 2020, https://www
.heritage.org/progressivism/commentary/feeling-guilty-about-everything
-thank-critical-race-theory.

5. Jonathan Butcher and Mike Gonzalez, "Critical Race Theory, the New Intolerance, and Its Grip on America," The Heritage Foundation, December 7, 2020, https://www.heritage.org/civil-rights/report/critical-race-theory-the-new-intolerance-and-its-grip-america.

6. Lily Sun and William Huang, "CRT Shares the Same Ideology as China's Cultural Revolution, Chinese American Warns," The Epoch Times, August 4, 2021, https://www.theepochtimes.com/crt-shares-the-same-ideology-as-chinas-cultural-revolution-chinese-american-warns_3930826.html.

7. Benjamin Wiker, "Darwin Nietzsche, and Hitler: Evolution of the Übermensch," Discovery Institute, May 13, 2008, https://www.discovery.org/a/5341.

8. Mike Gonzalez, "The Agenda of Black Lives Matter Is Far Different from the Slogan," The Heritage Foundation, July 3, 2020, https://www.heritage.org/progressivism/commentary/the-agenda-black-lives-matter-far-different-the-slogan.

9. Mark Moore, "BLM leader: If change doesn't happen, then 'we will burn down this system,'" New York Post, June 25, 2020, https://nypost.com/2020/06/25/blm-leader-if-change-doesnt-happen-we-will-burn-down-this-system.

10. Joshua Rhett Miller, "BLM site removes page on 'nuclear family structure' amid NFL vet's criticism," New York Post, September 24, 2020, https://nypost.com/2020/09/24/blm-removes-website-language-blasting-nuclear-family-structure.

11. Yaron Steinbuch, "Black Lives Matter co-founder describes herself as 'trained Marxist,'" New York Post, June 25, 2020, https://nypost.com/2020/06/25/blm-co-founder-describes-herself-as-trained-marxist/.

12. Natalie O'Neill, "Black Lives Matter co-founder Patrisse Cullors resigns amid controversy," New York Post, May 27, 2021, https://nypost.com/2021/05/27/black-lives-matter-co-founder-patrisse-cullors-resigns-amid-controversy.

13. Elizabeth Matory, "Yes, There's a Problem With BLM, and No, You're Not a Racist For Thinking That," Townhall.com, September 30, 2020, https://townhall.com/columnists/elizabethmatory/2020/09/30/yes-theres-a-problem-with-blm-and-no-youre-not-a-racist-for-thinking-that-n2577207.

14. Council on Foreign Relations, "About CRF," CFR.org, https://www.cfr.org/about.

15. President George H. W. Bush, "The other 9/11: George H.W. Bush's 1990 New World Order speech," The Dallas Morning News, September 8, 2017, https://www.dallasnews.com/opinion/commentary/2017/09/08/the-other-9-11-george-h-w-bush-s-1990-new-world-order-speech.

16. William Jasper, "CFR: Still the Power Behind the Throne," The New American, June 7, 2021, https://thenewamerican.com/cfr-still-the-power-behind-the-throne.

17. Jeffress, July 30, 2021.

18. Charisma News Staff, "CN Morning Rundown: Jack Hibbs: The Deception Jesus Talked About Is Here—Right Now," CharismaNews.com, August 5, 2021, https://www.charismanews.com/us/86305-cn-morning-run down-jack-hibbs-the-deception-jesus-talked-about-is-here-right-now.

Chapter 8 Politics and Media: Age of Deception

1. David Kupelian, "The gods of gaslighting," *Whistleblower*, December 2021.

2. Carl von Clausewitz, *On War* (1832–34), bk. 8, ch. 6, sect. B, https://www.oxfordreference.com/view/10.1093/acref/9780191843730.001.0001/q-oro-ed5-00003050.

3. Dr. Thomas Horn and Terry James, *Antichrist and the Final Solution: The Chronology of the Future Finally Unveiled* (Crane, Missouri: Defender, 2020), 25.

4. Robert Black, *The Quotes of Robert Black*, Kindle edition (Snake Scorpion Press, 2020), quote #1308.

5. Amy Watson, "Share of adults who trust news media most of the time in selected countries worldwide as of February 2021," Statista, June 2021, https://www.statista.com/statistics/308468/importance-brand-journalist-creating-trust-news.

6. Matt Taibbi, "The Media's 10 Rules of Hate," *The Washington Spectator*, July 7, 2019, https://washingtonspectator.org/taibbi-10rulesofhate.

7. Jeffress, July 30, 2021.

8. Victius Maximus, "The Roman Soldier's Belt: Balteus or Cingulum Militare," The Romans in Britain, https://www.romanobritain.org/8-military/mil_roman_soldier_belt.php.

Chapter 9 Education: Indoctrination and Propaganda

1. History.com Editors, "Great Purge," March 15, 2018, https://www.history.com/topics/russia/great-purge.

2. Dariusz Tolczyk, *See No Evil: Literary Cover-Ups and Discoveries of the Soviet Camp Experience* (New Haven, Conn.: Yale University Press, 1999), 19.

3. Mary Ann Peluso McGahan, August 13, 2021, Zoom interview with Troy Anderson.

4. Ibid.

5. Matt Bennett, "The Bible's Influence: Making comeback at Ivy Leagues," *The Washington Times*, December 11, 2014, https://www.washingtontimes.com/news/2014/dec/11/the-bibles-influence-making-comeback-at-ivy-league.

6. Ibid.

7. Alex Newman, "How John Dewey Used Public 'Education' to Subvert Liberty," *The Epoch Times*, February 26, 2020, https://www.theepochtimes.com/how-john-dewey-used-public-education-to-subvert-liberty_3116181.html.

8. *Britannica*, s. v., "School District of Abington Township v. Schempp" by the Editors of *Encyclopaedia Britannica*, accessed September 3, 2021.

9. Alex Newman, August 30, 2021, Zoom interview with Troy Anderson.

10. Ibid.

11. Ibid.

12. Seema Mody, "Millennials lead shift away from organized religion as pandemic tests Americans' faith," MSNBC.com, December 29, 2021, https://www.cnbc.com/amp/2021/12/29/millennials-lead-shift-away-from-organized-religion-as-pandemic-tests-faith.html.

Chapter 10 Intellectual Deception: Technology, Evolution and UFOs

1. Staff, "How Modern Weapons Changed Combat in the First World War," Imperial War Museums, https://www.iwm.org.uk/history/how-modern-weapons-changed-combat-in-the-first-world-war.

2. *Britannica*, s.v., "World War I" by the editors of *Encyclopaedia Britannica*, accessed September 5, 2021.

3. Alexandra Ma and Katie Canales, "China's 'social credit' system ranks citizens and punishes them with throttled internet speeds and flight bans if the Communist Party deems them untrustworthy," BusinessInsider.com, May 9, 2021, https://www.businessinsider.com/china-social-credit-system-punishments-and-rewards-explained-2018-4.

4. Louis Casiano, "How China uses its massive surveillance apparatus to track its citizens, keep them in line," FoxNews.com, May 1, 2020, https://www.foxnews.com/world/china-massive-surveillance-apparatus-track-citizens.

5. Paul Mozur, Jonah M. Kessel and Melissa Chan, "Made in China, Exported to the World: The Surveillance State," *The New York Times*, April 24, 2019, https://www.nytimes.com/2019/04/24/technology/ecuador-surveillance-cameras-police-government.html.

6. Newman, August 30, 2021.

7. Ibid.

8. Ibid.

9. Staff, "Exulting in Science's Mysteries," *The New York Times*," September 19, 2011, https://www.nytimes.com/2011/09/20/science/20quotes.html.

10. Yonette Joseph, "Stephen Hawking, in His Own Words," *The New York Times*, March 14, 2018, https://www.nytimes.com/2018/03/14/world/europe/stephen-hawking-quotes.html.

11. Adam Gabbatt, "Stephen Hawking says universe not created by God," *The Guardian*, September 1, 2010, https://www.theguardian.com/science/2010/sep/02/stephen-hawking-big-bang-creator.

12. Ken Ham, "Were You There?" Answers in Genesis, July 15, 2011, https://answersingenesis.org/blogs/ken-ham/2011/07/15/were-you-there/.

13. Interview with David Berlinski, Stephen C. Meyer, David H. Gelernter, "Mathematical Challenges To Darwin's Theory Of Evolution, With David

Berlinski, Stephen Meyer, And David Gelernter," Hoover Institution, July 22, 2019, https://www.hoover.org/research/mathematical-challenges-darwins-theory-evolution-david-berlinski-stephen-meyer-and-david.

14. Hugh Ross, September 20, 2021, Zoom interview with Troy Anderson.

15. Fazale Rana, "Can Science Identify the Intelligent Designer," Reasons to Believe, July 16, 2015, https://reasons.org/explore/publications/articles/can-science-identify-the-intelligent-designer.

16. Ross, September 20, 2021.

17. Mark Clark, "New US Government UFO Report: A Christian Perspective," Reasons to Believe, August 12, 2021, https://reasons.org/explore/blogs/voices/new-us-government-ufo-report-a-christian-perspective.

18. Julian E. Barnes and Helene Cooper, "U.S. Finds No Evidence of Alien Technology in Flying Objects, but Can't Rule It Out, Either," *New York Times*, September 1, 2021, https://www.nytimes.com/2021/06/03/us/politics/ufos-sighting-alien-spacecraft-pentagon.html.

19. Clark, "New US Government UFO Report."

20. Ross, September 20, 2021.

21. Ibid.

22. Derek P. Gilbert and Josh Peck, *The Day the earth Stands Still: Unmasking the Old Gods Behind ETs, UFOs & the Official Disclosure Movement*, (Crane, Mo.: Defender, 2017), 1–2.

23. Derek Gilbert, in-person interview with Col. David Giammona and Troy Anderson at Hear the Watchmen's "The Warriors Conference" in San Diego, California, September 18, 2021.

24. Dr. I. D. E. Thomas, *The Omega Conspiracy: Satan's Last Assault on God's Kingdom* (Crane, Mo.: Anomalos Publishing House, 2008), 7–8, 23–24.

25. Thomas, *Omega Conspiracy*, 23.

26. Thomas, *Omega Conspiracy*, 24.

27. Ross, September 20, 2021.

28. Evans, September 22, 2021.

29. Dr. Danny R. Faulkner, "Does the Vatican Have a Telescope Called LUCIFER?" Answers in Genesis, March 2, 2019, https://answersingenesis.org/astronomy/does-vatican-have-telescope-called-lucifer.

30. Evans, September 22, 2021.

Chapter 11 The Hollywood Deception

1. Wayne Lonstein, "'Pay No Attention To That Man Behind The Curtain': Technology vs. Transparency," *Forbes*, November 8, 2017, https://www.forbes.com/sites/forbestechcouncil/2017/11/08/pay-no-attention-to-that-man-behind-the-curtain-technology-vs-transparency/?sh=10063d2f55d4.

2. Miriam Berger, "The new Star Wars movie shows two women kissing. Singapore cut the scene," *The Washington Post*, December 24, 2019, https://www.washingtonpost.com/world/2019/12/24/new-star-wars-movie-shows-two-women-kissing-singapore-cut-scene.

3. David Betancourt, "The story of how Superman came out as bisexual: It 'makes perfect sense,' *The Washington Post*, November 16, 2021, https://www.washingtonpost.com/arts-entertainment/2021/11/16/superman-bisexual-comic-jon-kent/.

4. John Anderer, "Survey: The Average Person Will Watch More Than 78,000 Hours Of TV," StudyFinds.org, December 2, 2019, https://www.studyfinds.org/survey-the-average-adult-will-watch-more-than-78000-hours-of-tv.

5. Merriam-Webster Dictionary, "Deep State," https://www.merriam-webster.com/dictionary/deep%20state.

6. Nicholas Schou, "How the CIA Hoodwinked Hollywood," *The Atlantic*, July 14, 2016, https://www.theatlantic.com/entertainment/archive/2016/07/operation-tinseltown-how-the-cia-manipulates-hollywood/491138.

7. Daniel Estulin, *Tavistock Institute: Social Engineering the Masses* (Walterville, Ore.: Trine Day, 2015), 1, 133.

8. Ibid., 1.

9. Ibid., 2, 211–231.

10. Ibid., 1.

11. Ibid., 142.

12. Sharon K. Gilbert as quoted in Thomas R. Horn, *Zeitgeist 2025: Countdown to the Secret Destiny of America* (Crane, Mo.: Defender, 2021), 178–79.

13. Ibid.

14. Newman, August 30, 2021.

15. Evans, September 22, 2021.

16. David Heavener, September 18, 2021, in-person interview at Hear the Watchmen's "The Warriors Conference" with Col. David Giammona and Troy Anderson.

17. Matthew Alford, "Washington DC's role behind the scenes in Hollywood goes deeper than you think," Independent, September 3, 2017, https://www.independent.co.uk/voices/hollywood-cia-washington-dc-films-fbi-24-intervening-close-relationship-a7918191.html.

18. Schou, "How the CIA Hoodwinked Hollywood," *The Atlantic*, July 14, 2016, https://www.theatlantic.com/entertainment/archive/2016/07/operation-tinseltown-how-the-cia-manipulates-hollywood/491138.

19. David Heavener, September 18, 2021, in-person interview at Hear the Watchmen's "The Warriors Conference" with Col. David Giammona and Troy Anderson.

20. Ibid.

Chapter 12 The Elijah Principle

1. SLMA staff, "The Science of STRESS," South Louisiana Medical Association, https://www.slma.cc/the-science-of-stress.

2. Lydia Saad, "Record Few Americans Believe Bible Is Literal Word of God," Gallup, May 15, 2017, https://news.gallup.com/poll/210704/record-few-americans-believe-bible-literal-word-god.aspx.

3. Jeffress, July 30, 2021.

4. Ibid.

5. Fr. William Saunders, "The Catholic Church and Abortion," Catholic News Agency, https://www.catholicnewsagency.com/resource/55397/the-catholic-church-and-abortion.

6. McGahan, August 13, 2021.

7. Ibid.

8. Evans, September 22, 2021.

9. Ibid.

Chapter 13 The Battlespace of the Mind

1. Staff, "Air Force Doctrine Document (AFDD) 1, Air Force Basic Doctrine," U.S. Air Force, September 1997, 79.

2. Derek Gilbert quoted in Paul McGuire and Troy Anderson, *Trumpocalypse: The End-Times President, a Battle Against the Globalist Elite, and the Countdown to Armageddon* (New York: FaithWords/Hachette Book Group, 2018), 115.

3. International Standard Bible Encyclopedia Online, "Mind," https://www.internationalstandardbible.com/M/mind.html.

4. Staff, BibleRef.com, "Hebrews 4:12 Parallel Verses," https://www.bibleref.com/Hebrews/4/Hebrews-4-12.html.

5. Pickern, July 19, 2021.

6. Evans, September 22, 2021.

7. Ibid.

8. Ibid.

Chapter 14 Family and Society

1. Brenda Vuleta, "Divorce Rate in America [35 Stunning Stats for 2021]," Legal Jobs, January 28, 2021, https://legaljobs.io/blog/divorce-rate-in-america.

2. Glenn Stanton, "FactChecker: Divorce Rate among Christians," The Gospel Coalition, September 25, 2012, https://www.thegospelcoalition.org/article/factchecker-divorce-rate-among-christians.

3. "Divorced or Separated Adults," Pew Research Center, https://www.pewforum.org/religious-landscape-study/marital-status/divorcedseparated.

4. Pickern, July 19, 2021.

5. Joseph M. Holden, March 21, 2020, telephone interview with Troy Anderson for a *GODSPEED* magazine article.

6. Ibid.

7. Ibid.

8. Cahn, July 30, 2020.

Chapter 15 What Right Looks Like

1. Evans, September 22, 2021.

Chapter 16 Avoiding End-Times Pitfalls

1. Bernis, October 22, 2021.
2. Jeffress, July 30, 2021.
3. Ibid.
4. Staff, "Jim Elliot: Story and Legacy," Christianity.com, https://www .christianity.com/church/church-history/timeline/1901-2000/jim-elliot-no -fool-11634862.html.

Conclusion: Be One of the Few

1. Tertullian.org, "On the Prescription of Heretics," https://www.tertullian .org/articles/bindley_test/bindley_test_07prae.htm.

U.S. Army chaplain **Colonel David J. Giammona** retired in 2018 after 32 years of military service. He is an end-times expert, scholar, author, writer and speaker who is president of Battle Ready Ministries, equipping the Church to be warriors for God in the end times. Find out more at davidjgiammona.com and battle-ready.org.

Troy Anderson is a Pulitzer Prize–nominated investigative journalist and the bestselling co-author of *The Babylon Code*, *Trumpocalypse* and *The Military Guide to Armageddon*. He is the executive editor of The Return International and the vice president of Battle Ready Ministries. He also writes for Reuters, Newsmax, Townhall and other media outlets. Find out more at troyanderson.us and prophecyinvestigators.org.

More from
Col. David J. Giammona
and Troy Anderson

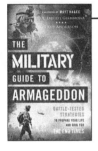

We are at war right now. The forces of light and darkness are lined up in battle array as the end of the age moves closer. Using both military and spiritual warfare tactics, this U.S. Army colonel and chaplain fully equips you to walk in the supernatural power and protection of the Holy Spirit as world events and biblical prophecies collide.

The Military Guide to Armageddon